CIRCLE AROUND MONADNOCK

Time Travel with Horses

Francelia Mason Clark

with

Pam Godin and Shelley Mozier

BAUHAN PUBLISHING
Peterborough · New Hampshire
2018

ISBN 978-0-87233-252-2

Library of Congress Cataloging-in-Publication Data
Names: Clark, Francelia Mason, 1938- author. | Godin, Pam, author. | Mozier, Shelley, author.
Title: Circle around Monadnock : time travel with horses / Francelia Mason Clark with Pam Godin and Shelley Mozier.
Description: Peterborough, New Hampshire : Bauhan Publishing, [2018] | Includes bibliographical references.
Identifiers: LCCN 2017049178 | ISBN 9780872332522 (alk. paper)Subjects: LCSH: Clark, Francelia Mason—Travel. | Monadnock, Mount (N.H.)—Description and travel. | Cheshire County (N.H.)—Description and travel. | Cheshire County (N.H.)—History, Local. | Horsemen and horsewomen—New Hampshire—Biography. | Women--New Hampshire—Biography. | Cheshire County (N.H.)—Biography.
Classification: LCC F42.C5 C55 2017 | DDC 917.42/904—dc23LC record available at https://lccn.loc.gov/2017049178

Other titles by or with Francelia M. Clark:
Theme in Beowulf and in Oral Epic, New York and London: Garland Publishing, 1995
Lake Nubanusit (Long Pond/Great Pond): Its History and Its People with Dave Robinson and Alison Rossiter, Lake Nubanusit Association, 2000
Time Travel With Horses: Exploring Early New Hampshire Roads From Peterborough to the Connecticut River with Pam Godin, Hollis, NH, 2007
Beowulf: A Performance Translation by Sebastian Lockwood and Francelia Clark, Amazon, 2017

Text and cover design by Henry James and Cassie Baron
Text set in Arno Pro with Seria Sans captions
Cover photo composite: Jaffrey Historic District Commission, Shelley Mozier, and Pam Godin.
Photo on the last page by Pam Royce

BAUHAN PUBLISHING LLC
PO BOX 117 / 44 MAIN STREET PETERBOROUGH NEW HAMPSHIRE 03458
603-567-4430
WWW.BAUHANPUBLISHING.COM

Printed in the United States of America

CIRCLE AROUND MONADNOCK

Reservoir
Beech Hill
Hurricane Hill
Dark Pd
1564
Dublin Pond
Dublin
BM 1439
Spaulding Hill
1545
DUBLIN GOLF CLUB
BM 1350
1482
LAKE RD
SNOW HILL RD
Sunset Hill
OLD MARLBOROUGH RD
LEARNED RD
D U B L I
1789
Hinds Bk
1491
CLOSE RD
OLD TROY RD
1449
FARMERS TRAIL
Mills
OXBOW RD
1344
Gleason Bk
PUMPELLY TRAIL
1214
PAGE RD
Brook
1313
MARLBORO TRAIL
MONADNOCK MTN
3165
FIRE LOOKOUT
WHITE DOT TRAIL
RED CROSS TRAIL
CASCADE LINK
HARLING TRAIL
Gilson Pd
Thorndike Pond
MOUNTAIN RD
SHAKER FARM RD
WHITE ARROW TRAIL
Halfway House
UPPER JAFFREY RD
GILSON RD
GIBBS RD
MCCOY RD
1366
Poole Res
Perkins Pd
BM 1249
Fassett
OLD KEENE RD
1159
Brook
1509
OLD MILL RD
J A F F R E
WHITES PATH
Whites Pd
BM 1097
1257
Cummings Meadow
1220
MILLIKEN RD
Jaffrey
1126
Mead Brook
Gap Mtn
1862
OLD COUNTY RD
GREAT RD
1246
Cubleigh Hill
Potters Pd
FITZWILLIAM RD
1275
1144
Gilmore Pond
1652
Hodge Pond
1160
Jock Page

CONTENTS

Monadnock from Gilmore Pond in 1910. Its southern slopes show widely open land.
[HISTORICAL SOCIETY OF CHESHIRE COUNTY]

PREFACE

The earliest settlers' roads in New England have long been concealed by forest or highway. But settlers on roads leave their marks. This book is a story of finding settlers' stories, of uncovering the old roads and signs of the old homesteads and their settlers in a particular landscape—but it could be another landscape.

This book is also about exploring a familiar region in a new way, first by foot and map, then in partnership with the trail horse for which the earliest roads were laid. Town histories evoked for us some of the detail of substance and suffering that went into living in this landscape. Then a settler's journal delighted and sobered us further.

There are survival stories to discover. A few of these early roads today have reversed their roles and become comparatively remote, as on Monadnock's forested north slopes. There, Shaker Farm Road still lies in gravel or dry brook bed, flanked occasionally on either side with the cellar holes from known settlers' original farms. Meanwhile, a group of earliest roads on Monadnock's southern slopes have been selected from the forest: they are now well-groomed trails passing oldest foundations with their own stories and long views.

Some early roads can still lead a hiker or a horseback rider over long distance—such as King's Highway, laid out in 1768, from Peterborough to Washington, and the traces of "great roads" rounding Monadnock. These have historic links to, at least, the long arteries made by traveling settlers and Revolutionary War soldiers. So certain bypassed historic roads, by means of some hunting, can still take us through countryside—with the discoveries that this entails. From such discoveries we have emerged full of admiration for the animal carrying us, respect for hard survival, and the urge to help others explore their landscapes in these ways.

A reader who knows horses may ask why an author who earlier rode King's Highway on a good black trail horse twelve years later rode the Monadnock roads on a Haflinger school pony, staying much more cautious, and grateful for two riding companions. The black horse might have told you that she and her rider actually were nearing the end of their story. Soon, she dramatically showed she had had enough, and was retired to a former owner. The recent Monadnock adventure underscores how lucky I feel today, albeit a widow, older, and quieter, to be exploring trails with this pony and these companions. It's a good sign for others.

—Francelia Mason Clark
November 2017

SOME WORDS ON A WINTER NIGHT

November 1, 1794

A comment floats into the darkness and cold, blowing rain.

"I can help you get to a horse to winter."

Captain Jonathan Hoar, the farrier, is speaking to the farmer Abner Sanger as they walk the two miles, and farther, from Dublin to their homes near and on Mount Monadnock's north slopes. Abner carries seven quarts of the last grist from his corn crop, ground at the mill after hours of waiting. Jonathan was at the mill to help reckon the price.

Abner has bartered for borrowing a work horse from Jonathan periodically across several years, with fair success. Ten days ago, Abner sent his eight-year-old son to another neighbor to ask for a horse, and that man sent the boy home on someone else's lame mare.

Jonathan adds, "I can get a horse of my brother in Marlborough."

They walk together. The rain hisses into sleet.[1]

SEPTEMBER 29, 2016

I have pulled up on northern Monadnock's Old Troy Road, riding my improbably beautiful palomino trail pony. We have come to that area in the forest, a gap in the stone wall, where suddenly I can see the cellar hole of Captain Jonathan Hoar. It is the granite basement of his home, where he was blacksmith, farmer, and father on this mountain 222 years ago. The weather is warm sunshine. My two riding friends subtly watch out for me, as does my well-trained pony.

We urge the horses a few yards into the trees, they bending a few sapling stems, so we can gaze into the home site. Two deep rock cavities enclose the substantial mound of a center chimney. The mammoth trunk of a sugar maple has grown into the far cavity. The dimension of this home was large, built for a family before the Hoars, and the size of the squared boulders of the walls and the foundation of the chimney show the house had a second story. Close around us in these woods the land is flat—perfect for a farrier's short-term holding of horses. We look at scattered boulders nearly buried in turf, trying to guess where Jonathan Hoar's smithy stood.

THE IDEA

What is the connection across more than two hundred years? Then and now, it begins with people encountering this mountain, which they will remember. Mount Monadnock in southwest New Hampshire, its sharp summit five hundred feet above the surrounding highlands, still "stands alone," as its ancient Abenaki name suggests. It dominates the horizon of people living in sight of it, orienting their view and affecting their weather. Its own weather is most reliably extreme: people report the summit as ten degrees colder, fifteen miles an hour windier, and distinctly more prone to fog and storm than its base plateau. Its slopes attract people to climb it—hundreds in middle nineteenth century, thousands today—except in winter. Hikers today are warned to respect the weather on Monadnock, and, in winter conditions, to stay away. Its local weather conditions are analyzed, storied, and never quite trusted.[2]

Unusual for central New England, Monadnock's land is preserved. Not only its bedrock summit remains open land, but most of its oldest climbing trails are intact. Some of its oldest roads are preserved as well, just where they were, now in deep forest. These roads were built to follow the earliest colonial homesteaders. For a while, beginning in the eighteenth century, communities of farmers were pioneering along the start of the steeper slopes of this mountain whose weather we do not fully trust. One might follow such roads. I began to yearn to try this.

And why would I want to? I grew up in a family of summer people, and so I climbed Monadnock, knew that my remote ancestors lived in its area, knew that its slopes held cellar holes of earlier people, and have always been attracted to its mystique. Add to it that when I retired from teaching literature to live in the Monadnock Region, I became a dedicated trail-horse rider, and the picture begins to take shape. Boarding my horse nearby, I was riding the mountain's lower slopes. The oldest trails kept heading farther up. Who would do that? The answer was eighteenth-century homesteaders. What was it like to carve out a farm, or to sustain a farm, on this mountain? Perhaps in part I wanted to understand my distant farming ancestors. Of course, from my distance of easy living I

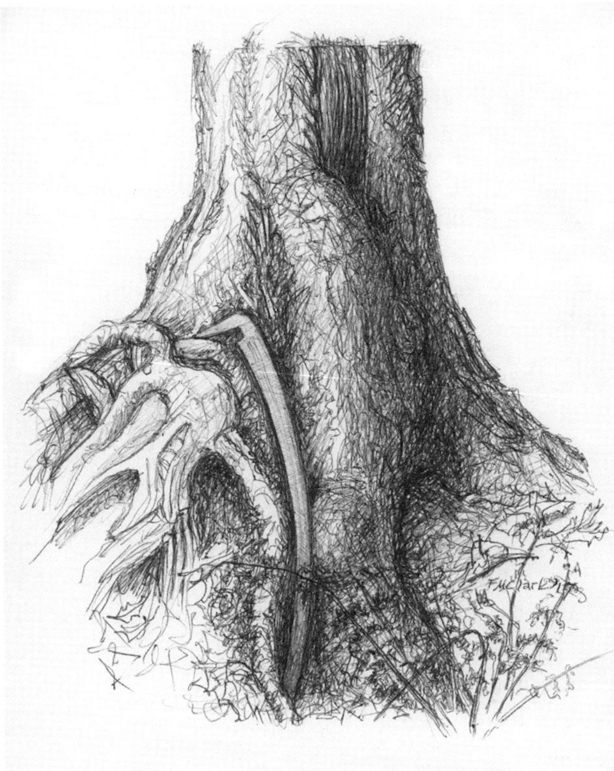

The Grass Scythe, 2017
[FRANCELIA CLARK]

could never truly know what it was like. Only those farmers could have known, among them Abner Sanger, who kept a journal. But if I wanted to learn something about it from a great cultural distance, an eighteenth-century journal and an eighteenth-century pack animal—a good trail pony—might be my envoys.

So I began to follow my curiosity, first into the readings. I wondered what were people's earliest records of being on the mountain. Did it sustain them? Apparently it did. Monadnock's first human record belongs to the Abenaki Indians. Abenaki history is not scripted; it is, however, engraved. On a flat boulder, on a mountaintop in Surry, is a large rock carving of a drawn bow, with three arrows in place and a grid of lines below. The bow bends toward Mount Monadnock, which, as Abenaki historian Marge Bruchac points out, was the center of this region for her people as well as for our own.[3] The Abenaki presence continually appeared for the earliest colonial soldiers and explorers, who arrived on the mountain in 1725 under the command of Captain Samuel Willard. Yet the soldiers' record book describes the signs as "old."

> [July] 30 . . . Found two wigwams made last year . . . also found a paddle and some squash shells in one of them. August the 1st . . . Found two wigwams made in June or July, as we suppose, and found sixteen of their spits which they roast their meat with, all in said wigwam . . .[4]

Yes, hunting and camping on the mountain gave the Abenaki part of their sustenance. Bruchac also depicts their response to colonial settlement in this area as a general drawing back, reluctantly making room, and staying unobtrusive as long as new treaties and boundaries were not transgressed. As we know, there was not enough room, or good will, for this to last.

Then, what do people generally know about "what it was like" during colonial settlement in the Monadnock area? The town histories have given us the outline of it. In the earliest years, tensions kept erupting. Interactions between the colonial settlers and the Abenaki around Monadnock can be traced approximately within decades, and they feature wars. Certain dates and decades offer some context for each settler's arrival on the mountain, for each early cellar hole. As a part of the rivals in King George's War, starting in 1744, the Indians drove the colonists away from the mountain. They struck and depopulated Keene in 1746, and warned, then forced, evacuation of the earliest settlers of both Dublin and Jaffrey by 1753. Yet by the end of the 1750s all three areas were settled again, Keene in 1752, Dublin in 1760, and Jaffrey in 1759. The parents of journal-keeping settler Abner Sanger left, and then returned, to Keene during this period.

As rising colonial population and resulting tensions continued into what became the French and Indian War, ca. 1753–1759, armies were raised from the colonies, which gradually fought both French and Indians back. Many soldiers returned home only to infect other settlers and die of smallpox. But they had driven the Abenaki either out of their homelands or to "hiding in plain sight" (Bruchac's phrase)—that is, no longer dressing like Indians, and therefore no longer in sight within their homelands—by 1760. For the settlers, as Sanger wrote about the end of this war, "his war," to his son years later, it was at last "No more Indians coming down and killing." He had had experience.[5]

In the relatively quiet period between 1760 and the Revolutionary

War, the movement of settlers from Massachusetts into the Monadnock Region increased. Of the homesites we riders were to visit on Jaffrey's southern slopes of the mountain, the earliest families came in this period, about 1773. Then, partly because the new American government rewarded returning soldiers with land grants, the population multiplied. Of the homesites we noted in Jaffrey and Marlborough on the western and northern slopes, two families arrived in 1778, finding another family already long settled. In the 1780s three more families whose farm sites are still visible moved onto Dublin's northern slopes. Now the settlements of the region began to stabilize. Those farmers who made it began to add onto their cabins, or build anew, with double stories. By the 1790s Keene and Peterborough were stable towns. The villages of Jaffrey and Dublin were incorporated. Mills and farms were expanding. Roads extended between settlements, and some houses became taverns. All along this way, the slopes of Monadnock kept looking very attractive to new settlers. Parts of the mountain's higher, difficult roads became more settled, for a while, than they ever would be again.

That brings out what puzzled me. As Jaffrey and Dublin came to provide more stable living, some people still moved to live higher on the mountain. I was not inclined to try to do research into why they came. But there are some written records from these same people, while they were living here. So my curiosity drew me into a different landscape and way of life. Knowledge and support began to come from conversations with people who know farming. It came from the respective town histories of Dublin, Jaffrey, and Marlborough, and from the published studies of Monadnock. But vivid details of life began to come particularly from two lucky sources: a current specialist in the cellar holes of farm dwellings on the mountain; and the relic, *Very Poor and of a Lo Make: The Journal of Abner Sanger*, a personal record of farming in western Dublin from 1791 to 1794. Abner Sanger's farm was across a swamp from the main slopes of the mountain and only a bit removed from the village, but those slopes were remote, and this farmer worked steadily with his more remote neighbors.

There is a question of connection from another point of view. What made me think I should take any horse for nearly thirty miles circling the mountain on the eighteenth-century roads, some now private, most closed in by forest? Thirty miles is routine for a seasoned rider, but I am not that. I am a retired college English teacher, a senior citizen. I have never been a strong rider. But I have riding friends who listened, and then supported me in this idea. I loved these friends, my quiet trail pony, and the aim of a low-risk adventure. But there's more: "what was life like" translated most obviously into a very reachable hope of awakening a fuller first-person experience with a working animal. That is a bond, and it is a historic relationship, and I ride one of those animals.

Not only planning but scouting every route was essential for me. I must scout if I am going to ride confidently. As for planning for the sake of landowners: on a mountain under continual pressure from tourists from everywhere in the world, we would make no friends by simply arriving on horses to charge through someone's shrubbery. I soon learned not to even think about reopening old bridle trails. Except for Jaffrey's Grand View estate, where I already had permission to ride, and two other permissions, I chose only the oldest remaining town roads for us. Initial meetings with historians and a town archivist helped lay out the options. Next came the scouting—walking the trail, usually with another person, to see if an option was actually passable. Then came required meetings with town clerks to go over the current property maps, even on a seldom-used road so that, with the good will of the town, I could learn of any problems with horses passing through. Finally came follow-up letters and phone calls for permission to trace a road through private land, or simply for good will if we should suddenly appear. These necessary experiences were in fact a pleasure as well as a help. Overnight stays at two antique inns, which I arranged months in advance, were a lucky and historic privilege—joyful punctuations in our ride.

In total, I wanted to ride for the adventure with friends, for increasing the bond with my pony, and, in part, to explore what seemed a puzzle about living. Monadnock appeared to have once held settlers who lived a contradiction: people chose to live on the land where the land was most difficult to live on. Could I learn something about the pleasures and ordeals of these farmers on Mount Monadnock? I could try.

So this writing traces a modest three-day horseback ride, circling by the oldest extant roads through Monadnock's southern, then northern, settlements, for the pleasure of it, for bonding, and to follow a curiosity.

DAY ONE

On the Eastern and Southern Slopes—Dublin and Jaffrey

Beech Hill
Hurricane Hill
Dark Pd
Dublin Pond
Dublin
DUBLIN GOLF CLUB
LAKE RD
SNOW HILL RD
LEARNED RD
Bixby Hs
CLOSE RD
D U B L I
Hinds Bk
FARMERS TRAIL
PUMPELLY TRAIL
Mills
School Hs #4
OXBOW RD
Bullard Site
PAGE RD
MONADNOCK MTN
FIRE LOOKOUT
WHITE ARROW TRAIL
WHITE DOT TRAIL
RED CROSS TRAIL
CASCADE LINK
HARLING TRAIL
Halfway House
Gilson Pd
Thorndike Pond
UPPER JAFFREY RD
GILSON RD
GIBBS RD
MCCOY RD
Woodbu Hi
Poole Res
Brooks
Ark
OLD KEENE RD
Hudson
Dole
Milliken Tavern
WHITES PATH
Whites Pd
Bailey Mills
MILLIKEN RD
Cummings Meadow
Stony Brook
J A F F R E
Jaffrey
OLD COUNTY

Pam Godin, Misty, Francelia Clark, and Shelley Mozier pose before loading in Hancock.
[AL STRUTHERS]

TUESDAY, SEPTEMBER 27, 2016

This early morning is our landmark. My friends and riding companions, Pam Godin and Shelley Mozier, and I are setting up in my converted garage in Hancock, New Hampshire, where I have been hosting our three trail horses in late summer. This morning we are about to follow my dream, and I'm feeling very lucky. For months, I have been scouting and asking permissions of landowners for a twenty-eight-mile, two-overnight ride around Mount Monadnock, following approximately the course of colonial settlements. For the overnights, amazingly, we have two remaining old inns, each with a stable—no longer do I want to camp out in a sleeping bag close to a snuffling muzzle. My friends know that I'm good for no faster than a trot, but they are still coming with me. And with them I know Misty, my pony, and I can do it.

The ride begins at the corner of Close and Upper Jaffrey roads, Dublin.
[JENNY WILLIAMS]

And now the thing is happening. We are all moving in a three-horse trailer, and I've been given the front seat with Jenny Williams, a horsewoman and riding school owner, and our driver today. On the map our riding "circle," moving clockwise around the mountain on the oldest extant roads, looks rather like a starfish, the outline angling from pavement to dirt tracks wherever possible. But it begins and ends at a sensible place. Jenny deftly eases the trailer onto the margin of Upper Jaffrey Road, in central Dublin, at its junction with Close Road. She sees us through mounting and snaps a picture of us at our trailhead. The weather, thick and gray around us, may lift or pour. We have chosen these particular days—early autumn, beyond heat and before frost, and in mid-week when traffic is low. But we will just have to cope if it rains. Shelley has found us one optimistic forecast, and we are simply willing that forecast to be correct. With a cheerful "Go easy, then," Jenny's off and we are moving.

The plan is to start the horses moving comfortably on a short gravel U-turn: west on private Close Road with permission, south and then east on Learned Road, to return us with a bit of momentum to the pavement of Upper Jaffrey Road. Our horses seem unbothered by the truck ride to an unknown place and they move out readily. On this gentle uphill gravel road in the woods, I give Misty the lead. After several yards, by slowing significantly she offers it to Jack, our usual lead horse.

Jack is a powerful Appaloosa trail horse, red roan with chestnut ears and mane, who combines size and strength with characteristically flawless obedience to Shelley. Our two horses board together. Repeatedly I have seen Jack's eyes soften when Shelley commands him. Jack fears nothing if he has met it before in his ten years as Shelley's only horse. He is most content when he is in the lead. So is Misty.

Pam's horse, Beauty, is a medium-sized red chestnut Appaloosa, with a white face, white speckled rump, and a blue eye. Beauty has spent eight years trail riding and fox hunting with Pam. Pam has been a professional trail-riding guide and my visiting trail companion for fourteen years, and I have shared a major riding adventure with her before, seen in our book of 2007. It is through a friend of hers that I had the luck of finding my trail pony. Reliable Beauty specializes in the most difficult land: bushwhacking and water crossings.

Misty the Haflinger, petite at 13.2 hands, came to me in a stroke of good fortune four years ago after nine years as a children's riding-school pony. The palomino breed of Haflinger was formed as a small Alpine working horse, and this shows. Misty has brightened my riding horizons because she is serene and willing, personable, lovely, and small. She is an excellent trail pony, even a caretaker, staying calm with almost everything—leashed dogs, trucks—as long as I do. As for the riders, we are all mature, but my friends work full time while I am retired. They are expert riders while I am good only if there is no emergency, so I focus.

We are very close to the mountain, but Close Road is named for a family whose descendants still live here. The road quickly gives us a vista of fields at the top of the rise, and our first meeting with history is elegant. A gorgeous, corniced white Georgian home renovated in 1902 comes into view ahead of us, with old oaks and a sharp summit view. This home, Mountain View Farm, was a retreat for Mark Twain for the summer of 1906. That columned porch appears in a photo of Twain in a rocking chair, looking out. Handwriting drifts down into the photo from the top. It says, ". . . and just put my whole *heart* in it. . . ."[6]

At this home, our way narrows and turns down-slope to meet Learned Road. The horses have relaxed into what we are doing and are just

Nathan Bixby's home of ca. 1780 became a preserved ell behind the Uptons' Mountain View Farm, where we see many guests before renovation in 1902. Below, recent owners keep Bixby's ell and Mark Twain's view from the front porch.
[HISTORIC RESOURCES INVENTORY, DUBLIN HISTORICAL SOCIETY]

swinging along; they are already being a pleasure. As they walk down, we have a long view through the foliage of descending fields in front of the mountain. Then we turn again, before another home, set well back. When I was scouting I found a small cellar hole just beyond us. It belonged to Abel Munroe, a "house wright" who may have built his own home in 1785, but he bought the lot in the year he was married, 1793. The cellar hole of his basement is small, but the house must have had substance: Munroe married his successful neighbor's daughter, Martha Bixby, and the house had two successive owners after him. Its foundation stones are large, cleanly cut and still squared, suggesting the quality of his craft.[7]

Most of Learned Road runs on as a wood-road, gated below our access. It is historic, lying roughly parallel to the Upper Jaffrey Road. It preceded Upper Jaffrey as part of the way people settled Dublin's eastern highlands below the summit. This neighborhood is one that they settled. On the map, the pattern resembles what is known about earliest New England colonial settlements. Earliest settlers did not care about commuting; they built paths, called roads, to their own homestead clearings and to their nearest neighbors, and if possible to a mill. So this short public spur of Learned Road, where we now head east to the pavement again, may have been built to avoid the course of a tributary of Hinds Brook, but it likely served to attach neighbors to a height where others were homesteading—or to attach those upland homesteaders to the path downstream to someone's mill.

We riders are surely not trying to find all of the cellar holes. But some of the settlers' names here are telling. Deacon Benjamin Learned came up from Sherborn, Massachusetts, to begin the family homestead in 1767. My own remote ancestor, Moses Mason, came up here in 1767 from Sherborn as well, beginning a clan that after a century totaled a startling number: nearly 350 Mason names are indexed in the *History of Dublin.* Loners paused here. During the Revolutionary War years, Willard Hunt from Holliston, Massachusetts, built a house on these slopes beside small Gilson Pond. With settlement increasing in 1800, and perhaps with signs of neighbors' discontent with his son Isaac, he moved his family off to Hancock, where they lived in the only house at the mill on Hunt's Pond.[8]

These open fields of Mountain View may trace back to Bixby's pastures.
[PAM GODIN]

With the journal from Dublin in the 1790s, and the help of a history of Dublin homes, we can see another dimension. It was to this road that Nathan Bixby, Revolutionary War veteran and blacksmith, town office-holder and tavern keeper, moved from a different lot in Dublin, in 1779. Extending behind the corniced white home that so attracted our attention is a wing, which I for one scarcely noticed. That wing was once an eighteenth-century farmhouse—Nathan Bixby's home. Once one knows, it is easy to picture his horse herd drifting across those gently sloping pastures. Bixby traded horses with the farrier Jonathan Hoar of Old Troy Road. These horses were called by the farmer Abner Sanger, who greatly needed them, the "Hoar/Bixby horses." Sanger bartered for them from Hoar, and they were often horses that were lame when they came to him. Bixby's herd must have included young and old and sound and lame both, for possible use.[9]

I begin to imagine: Bixby comes along toward us, sitting straight, riding one horse and leading another. The second horse, at close range, shows a slight limp. Bixby is heading into Dublin with a "bargain." —But then,

On the lawn that leads to Oxbow Road.
[EDIE POWELL]

what do I know about using lame horses in the frugal eighteenth century? According to Abner Sanger's journal, for him any living horse was hard to get. The histories show that both Jonathan Hoar and Nathan Bixby were respected citizens, who also owned pews in the church. Perhaps these so-common lame horses were useful because they were affordable for a poor farmer. I imagine myself in this role. As a poor Mason family member, had I bartered for a sound pony, I would have had to work her hard for every task beyond my strength. When she went lame I would have had to keep on using her. She then would have been a short-lived "old lame mare." Sanger helped people flay the carcass for leather. I, of course, would have needed shoes.

Now we begin to ride the paved Upper Jaffrey Road. It has margins quite narrow for horses, but in this fall season on a weekday morning, these horses are comfortable, easily passing along the edge of the pavement. To give us early confidence about traffic pressures anyway, my companions discreetly put Misty and me in the middle position, single-file. Each passing car gives the horses no reason to hesitate. Our morning is still gray and feels damp,

A rider's dream: Oxbow Road begins as a grass path.
[SHELLEY MOZIER]

but the horses are clopping along on dry asphalt lined with ferns.

After a scant mile we reach the left turn onto an old track I find haunting in name and in passage through: Oxbow Road. It begins much like a gravel driveway in the woods between spaced contemporary homes. But right away it offers history: the nearest one of these homes is built to enclose an old red schoolhouse, No. 4, of 1805. This corner had already been settled by 1772. The spot, then, could have been a settlers' focal point, a crossroads that had some children, was near a brook, had level ground with room for more distant people to gather, park wagons, tether a pony. It was, and perhaps still is, a social place: people living at this junction today take an interest in us, responding cordially to my letter that introduced us, coming out with a camera.[10]

"Oxbow," I have learned, refers to the great iron loop below the neck of each ox when the two are joined in a yoke. Indeed, the map shows this road as a large curve. At first our track runs straight off beyond the homes, a green aisle across a pasture. Then it eases under white pines on a soft pine-needle bed. When I scouted the way with my daughter in a light snow cover last winter, I learned to ignore a fork between walls that leads to cellar holes more distant from the mountain. Instead we head gradually downhill into a progressively older forest. The maps I have seen show no former dwellings here, yet there's a feel of them. We are moving through a canopy of old hemlock forest, with living and dead black trunks, some of them curved across the ground. In dim light we can see far among the trees. The earth around us lies in mysterious hummocks. The horses, however, are not peering around as I am; they move steadily on easy footing. We realize they are clearly having a good time.

In this lower forest, we are walking around milky puddles. But here is a big one, and Shelley and Pam let their horses have a long drink. I fuss around with Misty, wondering what's in this puddle, previewing that Misty will simply revive a former habit of pawing in the mud. But what could be more useful now than a drink? She drops her head; she's good. I get her out of it at the first lift of that front hoof.

We ride above a visual kink under this bow of a road. On the large curve, the earth drops steeply into a trough. But long bulwarks of rocks keep our road on a gentle descent. In deep forest, we are riding on an outsized curving embankment of rock, which passes us along solidly some fifteen feet above the gully. This was all hauled and placed by people and oxen at huge effort. Our puzzle is "Why?" The brook bed that flows under is very small: this is no mill. It's an openly worked and beautiful place. I have thoughts of railroad, of ancient aqueducts. But no, apparently this rock is massed up for sheer strength of an eighteenth-century freight road, once someone's major achievement for attracting steady draft-horse and ox-team traffic between living areas. Only this massive embankment, over a steep dip in a road, shows that the road was important.

Weeks later I learn why it might have been so important, from the Dublin hand-drawn topographic map of 1906. A discontinued road headed straight off from this masonry to busy mills on Stanley Brook, the reliable outflow from Thorndike Pond, and by that route those mills were only half a mile away.[11] They could have received all the settlers in the areas we have just passed. Reaching a mill would have been worth the huge effort.

On our track, we begin to climb out of this valley, the footing now slightly

Simeon Bullard's homestead of 1771, which Allen Chamberlain was seeing in 1936.
[DUBLIN HISTORICAL SOCIETY]

less firmly graded. We are traversing the side of a ridge, beside a wall with a steep rise on our left and a slant downward—a drop-off—on our right. The understory has returned, the trees are middle-aged birch and beech, and indeed we are passing posted signs that this land is still farm property. As the hillside rises the passage narrows between these slopes, and I have begun to look for a large fallen beech trunk all but blocking us. Last winter when we were scouting, I tried to imagine easing a horse around its roots at the edge of the slope—and I thought I could. Quite suddenly I realize we must have ridden past the spot: someone took the tree out without a trace. In the old days that kind of shaky estimate could have forced one to turn back, costing hours; in the wrong season, costing a night in the woods.

And so I am all but giddy with joy in what we are doing as we finish this road. We pass through in a ditch just below Oxbow Farm, which has barking dogs, a potential threat to horses if they are loose, but they are electronically collared and we're fine. A lively brook must course down this slope that joins Oxbow to Page Road: its boulders and leaf dams are not good for horses, but it's short and we scramble out, doing just fine. My fingers are reaching between the reins to caress Misty's neck. "Good horse, good animal." Page Road has unlikely short, steep gravel hills passing around a Boy Scout camp, and these are easy. We have glimpses of

Thorndike Pond, and I know from an old photo that somewhere among those buildings not many years ago stood one of the oldest houses in Dublin, Simeon Bullard's beautiful old Cape Cod home of 1771, sheltered by one of the oldest elms in the region—but we can't have everything.[12]

What we do have is about half a mile of the pavement again, now called Dublin Road because we have crossed from Dublin into Jaffrey, and then a turn onto Gilson Road. Turning away from the pavement here means we miss a touch of the future: a rescue organization for Newfoundland ponies has bought an old farm ahead. I like to visualize a line of sable trail ponies with riders trekking along these same quiet roads.

We are trotting, with spirit. Shelley and Jack are keeping the pace exactly right. Misty has two trots, sewing machine and long, smooth: this is the long one—and so comfortable. Gilson Road is gravel, straight, and quiet. To me it is the living dream of a country road two generations ago, with well-spaced homes half concealed under old trees, vegetable gardens, bee hives, a pumpkin patch, and some yellow fields leading the eye toward sudden views. Though it was formally laid out to border Thorndike Pond in the 1890s "for development," that development stayed subtle. Researching Jaffrey's roads, Coburn Kidd observes that parts of Gilson

Monadnock appears for us from Upper Jaffrey Road.
[SHELLEY MOZIER]

The mountain's summit beginning to clear, from the Joseph Thorndike, Jr.,farm of 1775, McCoy Road, Jaffrey. [PAM GODIN]

Road must be the very old connecting network of roads we have been riding.[13] Now we can see the steel blue of a gradually brightening day on Thorndike Pond on the one hand, and on the other, here is just the beginning of a mountain. It's the lower half of Monadnock, dark and close and disappearing into a thick cloud. I see a perfect opening at the pond for the horses to drink, but having sampled the puddle back in the woods they are content to keep moving.

A broad wetland appears below and ahead of us, and we turn sharply toward the mountain. This is the gravel McCoy Road, and at first we enter a sort of green tunnel through mature oak forest. We are climbing up again. The oaks thin to broad highland fields and distant homes. As we reach a height of this spur of hill, which feels only slightly parted from the main body of the mountain, I know there is a dramatic view of the summit across a steep valley, but still we cannot quite see that summit, just cloud. Yet the day keeps brightening and we are rejoicing in the growing sunlight.

One of the great joys of long-distance trail riding for me is to experience a horse adjusting to it. Crossing one of the heights of this hill is Gibbs Road, another very old track on our route; a sign well in front of a home asks people to travel across the field until they have passed the house. Misty sees the opening in the stone wall and walks right through. Ordinarily she would ask to start eating this grass, sometimes very strongly. But today, though I'm ready for this response, Misty just keeps walking on steadily. She now knows we are in this for a long haul, and she's committed. She is ready for every turn, every new road, and seemingly everything on it. For me this sense of sharing a project with a pony is a kind of continuing ecstasy.

Settlers must have known this feeling very well. Characteristically, most settlers seem to have walked all the routine distances and, as they became more interdependent, used (or borrowed) horses, especially to travel long distances. Of course, "long distance" to a settler would be both out and back, as we shall see, at some twenty miles a day, or it could also be migration, of at least thirty miles a day, where a willing horse, or a horse that becomes willing, would be crucial. While my "long distance" now is about ten miles a day, that's plenty enough for the bond between Misty and me to strengthen, and for me to be grateful for it.

To get to this high lookout, venerable Gibbs Road has angled up a steep washout. I rejected that slope, but that was the straightest part of this track, the earliest one connecting the two villages. According to Coburn Kidd, Gibbs Road was "not only the main route to Dublin, for a few years it was the only road." Gibbs was laid partially from the Dublin end in 1764, and the remainder through here from Jaffrey in 1775. That again shows earliest settlers' lack of routine travel needs. If one needed to ride back to one's down-country roots, as to fetch a bride, one had to travel from farm to farm. If one needed to go to war, one marched—walking fast in a group through farms and forest toward some distant "great road."

So the majestic white home before us with the helpful sign, so beautifully located on this height, had been a home in some form for two previous families across at least five years when landowner Joseph Thorndike, Jr., took it over and in 1775 achieved a road built by the town, which actually passes the house to somewhere else. Later, the home was chosen by the namesake McCoy family and enlarged by a succession of families since. Once, the Gibbs family lived just down the way.

For us, detouring slightly through the sweeping hillside field is a joy.

Luncheon for six, beside Gibbs Road.
[SHELLEY MOZIER]

Now in sunshine we all pass through Misty's gap in the long stone wall, across deep grass to a second field through another gap in the wall, and then in sloping grass toward a third opening. The horses reenter onto a dirt track, just beyond the Thorndike house and porch, leading down into a thin woodland.

The long, wooded slope, mildly stony, descends to an old sandy causeway across wetlands. Saplings line the causeway, with glittering views of the marshy brook to the left and right, yet the present drought has made our path comfortably dry. This place has not been waiting idly for our passage: we are following wheel tracks, and here are another horse's hoofprints. Soon we are trotting easily along this straight, soft, lovely track. After a gentle rise our trail becomes a year-round gravel road, complete with a driveway and distant house. But close beside us is an opening to a green field, empty and secluded, with a small conservation easement sign. Pam and Shelley know it's lunchtime, and have no trouble persuading me that this surprise is exactly what all six of us need.

We ride right in, dismount, and Pam quickly does me the favor of

slipping Misty's bridle out from under the trail halter and off for grazing. Shelley appears at my elbow with one of three large, fragrant ham and salad sandwiches. In this beautiful spot, the six of us relax, all eating lunch.

I think there's something about telling a horse, after a long ride and the beginning of grazing, to stop eating now and carry one off again—something that invites "No." I'm standing on a convenient stump trying to mount, and Misty, who knows better, keeps on moving, taking just one step to either side. She will not stand still. —And *will* not. Pam on Beauty swings over directly in front of us, broadside to the muzzle. Misty lets me mount.

Soon we are at another old corner. Gibbs Road empties between houses back onto Dublin Road, now close to Jaffrey Center. Somewhere on this corner is the empty site of another schoolhouse. But we turn back northwest, just a quarter mile, and the world changes before us. The view opens up to the biggest expanses by far: mowings, open hillsides, a round pond, a building, signs, and parking lots. It's the summer destination of the Monadnock Bible Conference. The building is a mass, a clapboard giant. That's the historic Ark, forty-seven feet by one hundred feet, vaguely hull-

On the road to The Ark, built by Joseph Cutter, Jr., in 1808, on Dublin Road, Jaffrey. Photos, respectively, show the 1880s and Jack in 2016.
[JAFFREY HISTORIC DISTRICT COMMISSION; SHELLEY MOZIER]

shaped, and given this name by an amused neighbor. It was built in 1808 by Joseph Cutter, Jr., in order to hold the ever-growing branches of the Cutter family of settlers.[14] By the time of the Ark, we have dropped into the burgeoning phase of Monadnock history, when there was a major freight and mail stage-team road over the southern slope of the mountain and through Jaffrey. Jaffrey Center in 1808 was growing into a lively town. Up higher on the mountain early, as well near here later, the individual cellar holes of the Cutters number at least six, and the family's contributions were making their members important citizens. For generations in Jaffrey, the Ark stayed well known as the Cutter family homestead and guest-house.

How well known? Consider: In the nineteenth century, Bible study was commonly taught in country schools by questions to the children, who would answer in chorus.

> Teacher: "Who wrestled with an angel?"
> Children: "Jacob wrestled with an angel."
> In Jaffrey, they said, and who could sit here and doubt it,
> Teacher: "Who built the Ark?"
> Children: "Joe Cutter built the Ark!"

But we on our horses are tiptoeing off this road just before the Ark, out of the nineteenth and back into the eighteenth century. The Old Keene Road is one of the paths that followed the pioneers who walked out of the village area and up the slopes to find a lot to buy and a spot on it to settle.

When we clear the busy grounds relating to the Ark, we are riding on an earth road, a narrow, true dirt road arched by saplings. I knew this road three years ago and I'm looking for a larger tree with a battered wooden sign of a cross-country ski trail from the 1930s. But I see only signs that Monadnock State Park borders the road, and we have permission. Without a pause, the horses carry us across a stubby bridge over a small dry brook. The trees are now mature hardwoods, and the earth is dotted yellow with the first small birch leaves. As we begin to climb comfortably the land once more takes on that just-perceptible open feeling, even while in deep woods, that it is reflecting someone's work. Here are short walls, half buried at right angles. Over the roadside wall, are the ground contours slightly flattened? And then here is the unmistakable turn, complete with a sign saying we have reached the cellar hole of one of the southern slopes'

Joseph Brooks's cellar hole, 1773.
[JASON HALLIWELL]

first pioneers, Joseph Brooks.

We are looking at what was once the dug cellar of Joseph Brooks's home. Now it is a medium-sized depression amid boulders with an indistinct chimney mass filling the middle of it, all of this rounded and filled by time. A researcher of cellar holes, Jason Halliwell, perceives from this that the house was a "modest hall and parlor-style farmhouse"—that is, two rooms surrounding hall, staircase, and central chimney on the ground floor, and two rooms upstairs. Barn ruins between two dwellings suggest that father and son shared a barn.

Joseph Brooks was a fifth-generation American colonist, born in 1750 in Acton, Massachusetts, who married Abigail, perhaps a Cutter, and began their family in Jaffrey. He bought this lot from a Masonian Proprietor[15] in 1773, built their home and moved to it in 1774. He was twenty-four. He fought in the Revolution at Cambridge the very next year. He returned, their family increased, and he became an active farmer. He had a brook in a depression just ahead, and a view down the slope across this path. His farm was the reason for the path, and later for another path getting him straight to the mills to our south. He also held village offices and held a pew in the Meeting House. In 1807, after his wife's death, Joseph began to persuade his son Jonas, by now a young father, to move onto an adjacent site. Jonas and his wife Mary, after the last of their seven children were born on this farm, moved into the new cabin next door in 1813. Then in 1816 both father and son moved away to Dublin, perhaps because of illness, because Joseph died a few months later at age sixty-six. By 1831 the original farm had become one of Joseph Cutter, Jr.'s pastures. The historical sketches suggest a careful life: earlier, Joseph Brooks made plans for his public contributions and protection of his family; and later, for his family to help support him.[16]

This home site marks our start into the loose community that, however briefly, made up the settlement of the south slopes of Monadnock. The Road to Brooks that we are on was misnamed "Old Keene Road" as a guess by a historian much later. First it simply went this far. Soon, just beyond where we ride now, it would connect Joseph Brooks, and the newer neighbors higher above him, to the Bailey mill. Later, it connected them all to the Meeting House that was gradually being constructed at Jaffrey Center—the austere and beautiful one that stands today.

These settlers were no hermits. We know they saw themselves as citizens of Jaffrey, because they were contributing to it. They intermarried, traded skills, commiserated, and visited as a mountain community, but they held town offices, helped build the Meeting House, sat on piles of planks in it, and later held pews in it as Jaffrey people. How much did the community of their church mean to them? Apparently a lot, and the most fortuitous factor may have been their appointment in 1782 of their Congregational minister, Laban Ainsworth. He warmly engaged with them, worked the land with them, and drew them to Meeting for seventy-six years.

Our first glimpse, then, of what Monadnock settlers were like as a crowd is a moment of celebration. Ainsworth's eulogist, Leonard Tenney, writes that the parishioners staged a housewarming party in 1787 for young Laban Ainsworth and his bride, as he brought her to the home he had just built in his new village.

> He was married to Miss Mary Minot, of Concord, Mass., and with her returned on horseback to Jaffrey. Soon after entering the town they were met by a numerous cavalcade

> and escorted on their way; and as they approached his house, a long procession on foot led them forward, when, opening to the right and left, they received the beloved pastor and his bride to his home, with the warmest congratulations. Within the house, everything was in perfect order. Fires were lighted and tables were furnished in the most generous style; so the day and evening were passed in gladness and social delight.[17]

Of those we are following from Jaffrey's mountainside, every established-church family would have been there—the Cutters, Brooks, Baileys, Doles. Help and hospitality were integral to the connection of people. To survive, they had to connect. There were some rogues, of course. A bit earlier, the settler John Grout had stolen the reserved Minister's Lot by building his own house on it. It took letters to the Masonian Proprietors from some twenty-five settlers before, together, they forced Grout into lot changes. To keep their connection healthy, people had to have some social control. Possibly the Grout family were not celebrating here.

But before paths led to the church, they led to the mill. When we come to a steep rise, we know enough to turn through a gap in the stone wall, heading on one still-extant path of generations of settlers to the magnet in an adjacent area, the Bailey mills. This is a broad grass path, curving and recently mowed, at first bringing us up a short hill. We have entered history at two levels: the very old reaches the recent. When we ride out of the forest onto high land, we can see around us wide, pastured, hill-like ridges. The ridges, like ancient burial mounds, are tawny September green and very old, but not natural. They are the accomplishment of the pioneering settler family that was to dominate this area, the enterprising Baileys. The summer-mown pastures are recent history.

Abraham Bailey was the first. He arrived as a sixth-generation Massachusetts resident who was somehow commuting back and forth from Tewksbury to build his first house on a new lot and join the Jaffrey church in 1773. He was twenty-six, a musically and mechanically gifted builder. The lot he chose was on the confluence of two small but vigorous brooks—for good reason. He founded the Bailey saw and grist mill, the first crucial element of the upland community. Soon his father, three younger brothers, and a sister joined him on his lot, and the first Bailey Mill began to flourish so quickly that by 1774 Abraham was sawing lumber

The Royces' fields include Wesselhoeft Pond
and a view of the cone of the summit.
[PAM GODIN]

there to build the Meeting House. He served in the Revolutionary War, was Jaffrey Selectman, sang the pitch for the hymns at church, and kept building mill machinery and houses for about six years. Then, perhaps like one of his wheels, he spun away to build distant mills. He died elsewhere in 1838 at age ninety-one.[18]

These sweeping fields with their odd grass ridges and ditches, all heading down the long hill ahead of us, have made another beautiful physical change in our ride. What they are, or were, is buried water movement: old underground pipelines and conduits to gather more water for the ever-growing and thirsty Bailey Mills. By two Bailey generations later, there were two mills below us. They additionally ground grain, made furniture and wooden tools, and carded wool, and they were drawing on every brook on these slopes, by every means. The path had become the Mill Road, heading straight for a former hamlet once called Baileys' Mills, and several tracks converged on this one, including the one from the Brooks farm.

Just to our left we can see shallow, privately owned Wesselhoeft Pond in a fringe of trees. This is the place of history within close memory. Hidden above the pond is a cabin, a former summer retreat of a most recent outstanding figure who has now become part of Monadnock's history, Charles Royce. He was the farmer whose cattle have kept these pastures. He was also a significant guardian of Monadnock in several ways: a protector, a conservationist, and a rescuer of hikers, who knew the mountain very well and for years served on call for emergencies. Before him, the Royces were a family of protectors of the mountain. His grandfather, William Crumbie Royce, tall and composed in a photo of 1920, was an admired woodsman, guide, and knower of nature. He was also an expert horseman. His great-granddaughter, Pam Royce, confirms that William Royce did in fact ride his horse successfully up Monadnock onto the summit. The ride, inconceivable to us, was in about 1900, over the White Dot trail that Royce had helped to complete and mark.[19] Still, you would ask, given that granite summit, how was this possible? Earliest photos show that long after the fires on the mountain there were still old stumps standing on the summit near the end of the nineteenth century. The burned-over soil eroded away only over a long time, gradually leaving granite without soil that now only hikers can safely navigate. There is possibly one more testimony to horses climbing Monadnock:

Very quietly, a horse stands on Monadnock's summit along with the visitors.
[COLLECTION OF LEE WILLETTE]

very quietly, a horse is standing alongside the visitors, quite unsung, in an old photo taken on the summit, now in the State Park museum.

This small Wesselhoeft Pond with edges of marsh links us with the old history because even this was siphoned into a conduit to feed the Bailey Mills. We ride in to see, for a few yards, on a side path that passes the pond. There's a wood-duck nesting house in the reeds. At the outlet below the earth dam, here are the culverts that took the water when the pond reached a certain level.

Mill Road, sometimes as a gully, runs straight on down through the trees, but to one side before us, a cattle gate is newly wide open and welcoming. We ride diagonally down across the Royces' long open field,

The Cascade at Baileys' Mills. Abraham's first mill was at work in 1774.
[FRANCELIA CLARK]

the cone of the summit just visible over the heights ahead of us. The open lower gate returns us to the road. As we finish Mill Road we are riding parallel to Mead Brook, which is accompanying us to the mill site. We have arrived in about half a mile total, where the road ends with a bridge over the old mill outflow, meeting US Route 124. This autumn the outflow below us is a stream between rocks, but normally it's a dramatic and white rushing cascade. I recall that three years ago, Misty started toward the bridge, which vibrated slightly over the cascade, and I was relieved not to have to find out whether she would cross it. Today with an unstressed bridge, and because I know her much better, she would cross, but my goal is still the mill.

Standing here we can reconstruct the mill site. Downstream we can see the empty earth basin dug for a grandson Bailey's diversified wooden-ware mill. Beside us upstream is the massive stonework rubble of the main mill, which also diversified over the generations and was once rebuilt. Above that is the now-concrete dam. It leads across a dark, lovely millpond to a finely preserved brown Cape Cod house, considered to be Abraham Bailey's house. The house fronts on US Route 124, which is also historic, at first as a successful path connecting settlers across the mountain. After the Revolutionary War, it was an established settler and trader route between towns and on into Vermont, called The Mountain Road. By 1800 it was the highway, busily carrying streams of freight by ox and horse teams, sometimes in winter in long trains of sleds traveling together. To accommodate these crowds, it held clusters of taverns for trade anywhere between Montreal and Boston, in this area under the new official name of Third New Hampshire Turnpike. In this immediate neighborhood, the highway further reveals the mill fortunes of the later Baileys, for two adjacent estates on it today were originally their proud homes.

With these mills, the hamlet attracted a blacksmith shop, several more houses, and a tavern—a lively, noisy place, Halliwell comments, while its valley was becoming Baileys' Mills. The hamlet holds at least two eccentric stories. The first story, received by Chamberlain from Edward Bailey, the last of the family mill owners, is why the name Baileys' Mills lasted only a few years.

On a winter night in about 1801 two Vermont sleds from the freight traffic pulled up to shelter at the tavern. Loading back up on the next morning, one of the drivers found he was missing a wheel of cheese. He accosted John Joslin, the tavern owner. An argument arose that could not be resolved: the cheese was missing and nobody knew what had become of it. Now a reputation was at stake, and everyone at hand turned out to hunt, while tensions grew. Then someone suggested they consult a widely-known clairvoyant, James Ballou, who lived in Richmond, ten miles away. As Chamberlain puts it, this "was probably regarded as something of a lark and off they posted, every man Jack in the village."

While most of the village was gone for the day, other sleds came in to stop at Joslin's tavern. These newcomers asked the women cooking at the tavern why the village was abandoned, and were told the men were all off consulting with James Ballou. This was hard to swallow. A trader must have grinned as he concluded, "So this place is Ballou's City." In fact, James Ballou, perhaps very wisely, concluded that a half-wit child had stolen the cheese. This satisfied the questers, who rode home that night apparently at peace. Later they identified an unfamiliar rind dragged home by a dog.

The "Mineral Spring" of 1805 still flows.
[FRANCELIA CLARK]

But their reputation had preceded them home: the name Ballou City for this spot remains on most Jaffrey maps well into the twentieth century.

Several postscripts could follow this story. But for me, it is first this: a twenty-mile horseback ride to Richmond and back in winter snow was all in a day's work—or pleasure.

The second story grew a bit later, with familiar characters. By 1805, the same John Joslin, and David Cutter, one of the Cutter clan, were licensing a novel discovery, with the help of a physician and a lawyer, as the "Proprietors of the Monadnock Mineral Spring." There beside the turnpike, they had discovered what seemed to be valuable mineral water for health, so they built a large new hotel by the spring and began to advertise. People came. Joslin and Cutter apparently flourished for eight years, until they attracted Harvard's chemistry professor J. Freeman Dana, who visited in 1816 and published his analysis of the water. The water contained carbonate of iron, but in quantity so small "as scarcely could entitle it [to be a] *Mineral* water." The resort business promptly began to tail off, and the whole enterprise was gone by 1824. But this story has two results. One is that some of those old Jaffrey maps show the hamlet "Ballou

Riding beside White's Pond, a Bailey millpond.
[PAM GODIN]

City" as "Mineral Spring." The other is more current and pleasing: that same spring water still flows today, from the mouth of a small horizontal pipe in the Royces' field. It nourishes cows, and you can see it from the highway. The stories seem to round out the traces of immense personal energies, so lightly concealed in this quiet place. The energies attest to the whole way of life.[20]

We backtrack several yards around the mill foundation and turn our horses up a short, wooded slope to the millpond. For us it's an adventure to ride these horses up onto the path that would cross the dam to the notched gears that govern the spillway. When we instead turn north on this trail, we are riding the grassy border of White's Pond. The millpond water holds a tranquil double reflection of evergreens. We are taking White's Path, a narrow earth line into the former network of the settlers. From here to our goal for the night we are in Jaffrey's Grand View estate, which preserves the southern slopes in this whole area below Monadnock State Park. This lovely woodland and its old trails make up the one area that Misty and I somewhat know and I did not scout. Soon we are riding through a cathedral of old pines. Their needles have been falling and make a soft fawn-colored mantle around us. We come to a pair of wood and rail bridges at right angles to one another over Ainsworth Brook and Dole Brook. One is just as sturdy as I recall it, but the other is quite broken. Beauty carefully descends the bank and shows Jack and Misty, and the three riders, exactly where to cross the brook between the rocks. Briefly we ride uphill to the edge of one of the Bailey estates, then return after Beauty across the brook to our trail.

But what trail? Beyond the bridges, just ahead, is the open and splintered expanse of a timber cut. Lumber trucks must be why the bridge is broken. The ground is stumps and downed branches, and deep in twigs and chaff. There is no visible trail. There's nothing to do but try to get through this to wherever we can get our footing again. It can't be far, so we thrash ahead. The horses are game, and Misty is quite good at doing this, and still I keep coaxing "Careful!" as if it helps. But this is dangerous for them. We creep up a slope that looked promising but is not. It's open land but nothing is cleared, and the horses are feeling their way through a trashed porous surface. I'm both frustrated and embarrassed. Because the land is wide open, I have by now no idea where the trail should be. When I was phoning for permissions, how many people did I mention this passage to, with nobody happening to say, "Well, you know, your path is devastated." But then, I didn't ask. I remember I was told something in connection with the broken bridge. Did I listen? Apparently not.

Even the horses are no longer finding this fun. Jack, for one, has stopped. But so has Shelley. "I'm not interested in broken legs," she says. "We've got to go back across the bridge and the brook and start riding the highway." And I am recalling that my sense of direction is a useless gland, and that it's now near four o'clock and we are, after all, heading up an unfamiliar slope on Monadnock.

So we turn around, dismount, and thrash with the horses back toward where we got into this. Somehow along the way a remnant of the trail appears between two trees. (Could it be that Misty has moved to it?) We lock into riding that. It's brushy but it exists. Somewhere up the slope were two cellar holes of early Cutters, but—here we are on a trail, relieved.

The first thing I recognize is the abrupt return of the old pine canopy, and a ring of firestones marking a one-time Boy Scout overnight. This is now a narrow strip of forest, but it is exactly as it was, if it can take us through. Then through saplings I see the perfect kettle hole, the round pond created from a melting mass of glacial ice, now dry marsh but not timber-cut. I remember in springtime the whistles and twangs of peepers and green frogs. Nothing could look more wonderful to me. Soon in the woodland we are passing around the lovely wildlife pond that widens from Dole Brook. Two heron nests are still out there, topping pine spars, reflecting in the bright water. We cross the shady ford in the brook, all three horses effortlessly, and emerge from a small lucky trail onto a broad gravel trail of the well-groomed Grand View estate. Every trail regroomed by this estate was also an old one, and we have turned out onto a parabola shape that appears on every old map: the Road to Benjamin Dole's.

As we ride the great curve of this settlers' road we begin to see long fields sloping down to our left, and to our right the fork of an old thread of trail heading higher. At this fork is the site of the cellar hole of Benjamin Dole's nearest neighbor, Benaiah Hudson, 1779. Apparently, Hudson brought his wife, Dorothy Lawrence, and the younger ones of seven children up from Pepperell, Massachusetts. Four years later they were gone, and the Proprietor resold the lot. The house went on: abandoned briefly, it then hosted two successive families with several children, then was truly abandoned after 1832. Halliwell perceives "a modest, corner-chimney

Benjamin Dole's barn foundation and field, from 1773.
[PAM GODIN]

dwelling" and a very small barn with a faint ditch line from a spring and a likely field barn on the slope above, suggesting livestock.[21] What is visible from horseback is only the shallow L-shaped rock depression inside the foundation rubble, almost gone under time. The small and shallow ditch is the pattern of the remains of settlers' homes farther up the slope. We are finishing our day in the area of the highest mountain farmers.

At last, in late sun, we ride into the farm site of the settler whose place interests me the most, Benjamin Dole. Dole was the very earliest settler of this community, coming to the mountain from Lancaster, Massachusetts, in 1773 and choosing one of the highest lots. He was twenty-eight. His wife, Relief Thompson, was also of a family that would settle here. The couple brought two children and raised six more on the mountain. He was a cooper and a town tax collector, and he owned a pew in the Meeting House. Before the Revolutionary War, Benjamin and his younger brother John earned a reputation on the mountain as successful wolf hunters. They must have been in demand. During the Revolution, he and his brother fought for several years, including battles at Bunker Hill and Ticonderoga. Benjamin as a corporal marched with his army from Rindge, New Hampshire, to Saratoga, New York; John spent time as a prisoner of the English, then re-enlisted—and later was killed at Albany.

Adams' Corner marks the old Mountain Road junction on the Dole farm site. We will ride straight ahead to open land.
[PAM GODIN]

The whole southern valley where we have been rises
in this view up from the highway at Royce's lower field.
[FRANCELIA CLARK]

The road that we are on, the Road to Dole's, became one of those first paths that did in fact lead over the side of Monadnock. It follows that in 1788, when there were travelers on this road and before there were large crowds, the Doles obtained an inn license and took in mountain travelers. Then by 1791 the town improved the route by channeling the Mountain Road straighter and away from their road, and compensated the Doles. The effect may have been either the loss of their inn business or too many crowds in either case. To have served as an inn, their home, if not one of the larger two-story hall-and-parlor ones, probably had additions. These houses were not primitive. You can see some of them in this region today— restored, exquisite, and warmly used, as homes, as estates, or as hubs of private schools. This one continued as a dwelling during the 1800s. It and other dwellings on this corner of Dole's Road, which first led across the mountain, became known as Adams Corner. This house was still barely standing, abandoned, in the early twentieth century, and finally razed and the cellar hole filled in 1954. Its final distinguishing feature must have been the lilacs growing around it. After twenty-one years here, in

1794, Benjamin Dole divided his lot among some of several families of relatives, and moved over the mountain to Marlborough.[22]

His long, lovely view of the valley below us has been restored to an extensive field. Neighbors and travelers on horseback would have stopped here at the barn to the welcome of a big family. We look down the valley from his barn foundation, by now a three-sided granite open shelter facing this field. Its rear rock wall is built into the hillside just below our road, and from this wall the two corners make long right angles of rock tapering gradually down onto the field. This could have been the barn's large ground floor for keeping a wagon, a stoneboat to carry rock, and a traveling freight sled, or it could have been livestock's ground-floor walkout. With simple beauty and mass, it suggests to me both shelter from the summit's storms and strength, a focus of a homestead.

To me, this family did it all. As for Benjamin Dole, is there any further remaining sign of what he was like? Well, yes, actually there is a small anecdote, and it's in the *History of Marlborough*. It is from 1794, when Dole was nearly fifty years old, an "old man" and a new Marlborough resident. Charles Bemis writes that at Monadnock, a bear escaped a neighbor's dogs, killing one, and moved up on the mountain.

> Benjamin Dole, who then lived on the Phinehas Farrar place, near the foot of the mountain—and who, by the way, was quite a noted hunter—found that night what course the bear had taken, went home and made preparations for an early start the next morning, hoping to secure the bear before the hunters should get upon his track. He charged his gun . . . as soon as he could see in the morning, started off into the forest toward the place where he supposed bruin had hid himself from his pursuers. Some three inches of light snow had fallen during the night. As he was jogging along, and before he had begun to look for his game, he of a sudden came upon him. The bear was completely covered with snow, and the man was almost upon him before he knew it. Bruin, thus suddenly disturbed, sprang up, shook off the snow, and hastily pressed his way toward the mountain. His enemy was too much frightened to level and discharge his gun, and the bear escaped. Mr. Dole, who had taken so much pains to capture him, did not hear the last of his bold adventure for many years.[23]

Riding toward the Milliken Tavern of 1800.
[PAM GODIN]

From all this I sense a sociable, active man, both very competitive and very responsible, and with an outreaching sense of humor. He could take a joke, sometimes even the same joke—over and over. He settled and thrived, and he did it twice. He worked in many capacities and was not stopped by winter. He made his house a tavern when he could. He raised a big family, in both communities: in Marlborough, Dole was teased not only for his bear hunt but for the large number of his children. "An old man" at age fifty, which was Sanger's generalization about aging, appears relative. Then too, as visible parts of our ride, these mountain locations inspire me to begin keeping track of settlers' aesthetics. In the anecdote above, Benjamin Dole was living, at least for a time, at an even more beautiful spot than his last one—arguably the most beautiful arable spot, high on a knoll of the mountain.

Late afternoon has become one of those clear, gorgeous days, the distance seeming as etched as the foreground in late sun and deep shadow. I am sliding my hand along Misty's silken neck again. "Good girl. Good pony." She has done it. All told, we have come over eleven miles.

The Milliken Tavern of Jaffrey as "Proctor House," 1880–1905, and as Grand View Estate today, Mountain Road (Route 124), Jaffrey. To see the original structure in the rebuilt one, count five upstairs front windows from left.

[JAFFREY HISTORIC DISTRICT COMMISSION; THE MANSION, GRAND VIEW ESTATE]

We are finishing our ride on a long field-side trail, both the open land and our border of foliage pointing straight at a distant white house—the Milliken Tavern of 1800. Apparently, a prior house in the shadow of the mountain was rebuilt in brick to last by Alexander Milliken, in order to receive the new era of the long-distance freight-wagon turnpike. It did that and it flourished, was enlarged, and after generations as a tavern, large farm, elegant estate, and destination, it stands open today, the focus of the Grand View estate, still receiving wedding parties. We ride below the hillside of the tavern, passing right out of the Grand View estate to cross Route 124 onto an apron of pavement in front of what looks like a Quonset hut or an airplane hangar.

Here we dismount and lead the horses by the reins straight in through the office front door. We are in a totally empty and closed stable, and from the office we lead them clopping and echoing down the empty aisle and turn them into three good box stalls.

With some help, we brought in floor shavings beforehand, along with brushes, hay, grain, and five-gallon buckets of water. The late afternoon is still giving enough light through some windows. Quickly, then, the horses are untacked, fed, grained, watered, and well settled. All six of us are sound and fine; and Pam and Shelley and I have just been freed for a long sunset, a historic, entirely glamorous, inn, and a small celebration. At Milliken Tavern, Pam Royce welcomes us. She is the inheritor of the family tradition protecting Monadnock, and as manager she has enabled us to stay here on this weeknight between scheduled weddings. She suggests we simply choose whatever rooms we like. That frees us to explore.

The historic Milliken Tavern has been furnished over time in part by the estates it has graced. So its interior does not look like, for example, Keene's Wyman Tavern, which has been kept in slenderest colonial detail. Milliken is startling in its formal and sumptuous, comfortable beauty. The windows attract me. Because many of the long rooms cross-sect the brick building, large windows pour in light from both ends of a room. Mirrors reflect these windows, giving the impression of light from all directions. The inn faces directly upon the mountain, so almost every room lays open for an onlooker the stunning view of the summit.

At times through these windows, relaxing and exploring indoors and out, we are watching the setting sun. As we arrive we can see the whole

Sunset from Milliken Tavern.
[PAM GODIN]

peak above the foothills, bright, still holding its late afternoon greens and grays. Indigo shadows lie to the east, far below clear granite sunshine on the point of the summit. Gradually we are aware that the indigo has spread across the lower tree line, the gray is creeping up above the tree line, and the summit, still just as bright, is tinting pale orange. Pam comments for the three of us: "Stop, we are trying to hold on to this day." The shadows keep climbing. Now that the cone itself is the only shard of sunlight in the view, we can see that it too is fading, from russet to lavender. The lavender softens into shadow.

Eighteenth-century settlers chose this spot. For tonight, Pam and I both choose the second floor west-end master bedroom, in the original part of the tavern, clearly visible in a photo of a jolly nineteenth-century crowd here when it was called Proctor House.[24]

Our celebration turns to dinner. Shelley's friend Tim adds to all the other help he has been giving us by arriving with a well-planned crockpot feast of chicken and mushrooms, just what we most welcome, and the feast includes champagne. Milliken's kitchen is modern and totally equipped to host a crowd. In fact, we do receive a brief guest: Louise Meijer, one of my main inspirations for riding around the mountain, drops by to exchange

Paired hames rest on the tavern's kitchen mantel.
[PAM GODIN]

greetings. She often rode a Monadnock circle that included such higher-ground trails as the Parker Trail, until the State Park went "modern" in its view of horse travel. This atmosphere keeps feeling more to me like an inn might have felt to an early traveler: horses comfortably kept, the place, food, and evening elegant, the company excellent. Above us on the kitchen chimney mantel stands a polished pair of hames—the thick, curved wooden poles with brass rings that lay upon a horse collar to guide the reins through the harness of a draft-horse team.

DAY TWO

On the Southern and Western Slopes—Jaffrey and Troy

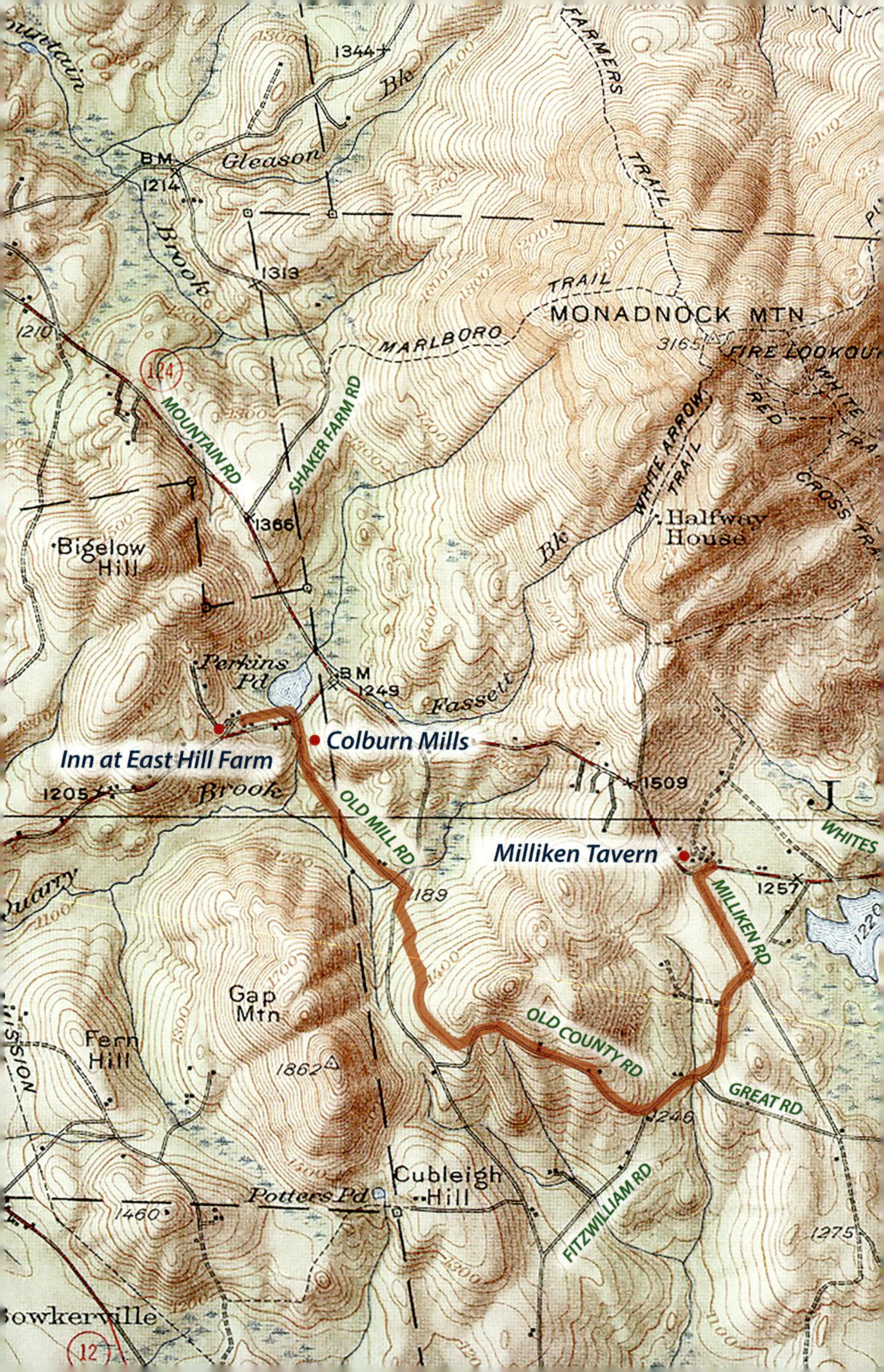

MONADNOCK MTN
FIRE LOOKOUT
3165
MARLBORO TRAIL
FARMERS TRAIL
WHITE ARROW TRAIL
RED CROSS TRAIL
Halfway House
Gleason Brook
BM 1214
1344
1313
1210
124
MOUNTAIN RD
SHAKER FARM RD
1366
Bigelow Hill
Perkins Pd
BM 1249
Fassett Bk
Inn at East Hill Farm
Colburn Mills
1205
Brook
1509
Milliken Tavern
WHITES
1257
OLD MILL RD
1189
MILLIKEN RD
Quarry
Gap Mtn
1862
Fern Hill
OLD COUNTY RD
GREAT RD
1246
FITZWILLIAM RD
Cubleigh Hill
Potters Pd
1460
1275
Bowkerville
12

The closed stable at Grand View.
[PAM GODIN]

WEDNESDAY, SEPTEMBER 28, 2016

The extremely comfortable night at the inn turns into a gray morning in a cloud. Pam provides coffee and bagels with all trimmings, and now her husband Leo comes by to greet us and take our (and our horses') duffels from here and the stable to our next night's lodging—a lot of help. Maybe after all we are shuttling gear between lodgings more like stagecoach travelers. But by day we ride the joy of warm living beings and our team is our own. All we have to do is get on and out.

Yet this foggy morning makes our unlighted stable aisle dark without detail. I lead Misty into the arena to "lunge," or exercise, her in a circle as I always do, but in this strange arena we both seem nervous. Now back with Misty standing, and trying to tack up with the saddle balancing on a window ledge between the arena and the dark aisle, I seem to be fumbling, a feeling of growing old right on the spot. At that moment Pam Royce, a lifelong horsewoman, comes into the stable to enjoy our departure and perceives exactly where she is most needed. She stands with my pony; my

Pam Royce holds Misty in the stable's arena.
[PAM GODIN]

pony and I relax; I can finish with the tack, and gratefully we can depart. We mount in the arena, riding this time right out the big arena doorway to Route 124. We clop across the highway onto a mowed margin, our last gift from the Milliken Tavern.

Milliken Road, a straight, ancient gravel extension from the tavern's driveway, takes us briefly south. It makes our circle wider, outside of the steeper slopes of the state park and the popular Half-Way House hiking trailhead. We are now on the margin of the southern slope community of Jaffrey, though still in the land of early settlers. We have a darker day, but a shorter riding day between the only two functioning antique inns at Monadnock. This road will take us on a passage that was opened earlier than any we have so far seen.

First, from this straight-arrow track, built to lead settlers living in Fitzwilliam and Rindge to and from Milliken tavern, we merge onto the Fitzwilliam Road, a grass-bordered pavement passing homes. Then—it's just a sign at a wide but empty intersection—Great Road joins us.

At first this seems unlikely to me. How many historical sources mention Great Road, and in how many locations? It seems always to be named as the earliest soldiers' treks from Boston to Fort Ticonderoga or Boston to Montreal. There is a historic Great Road immediately west of Boston,

We take Milliken Road, briefly south, beginning at the tavern.
[PAM GODIN]

where linked roads that head northwest, officially US Route 119, continually include its name. Keene's history claims a "great road": according to editor Lois Stabler, Abner Sanger had lived in Keene on the great road and had marched on it to the French and Indian War. Chamberlain claims it for Dublin, specifically along the south side of Dublin Pond and connecting to the Old Marlborough Road, where we will ride. Now we see that Jaffrey claims it as an east–west arc aiming to make a corridor for marching between Gap Mountain and Monadnock—once again a township's oldest road. These claims do not easily line up as a single route. We can at least see that none of them run straight over Monadnock's Mountain Road, but they all flow around the mountain, all of them indicating that the earliest brave soldiers marched to somewhere far.

The problem of the ubiquitous "great road" seems to be solved by Coburn Kidd. In this section of Jaffrey where we are meeting it, it's better known as "Old Fitzwilliam" Road, but its direction is significant.

> It may be part of the most venerable road in town . . . marked from Townsend to [Keene], laid out in 1735–36. It was variously called the Old Boston Road, Great Road, Main Road, Old County Road. Old Fitzwilliam lay in the right place.[25]

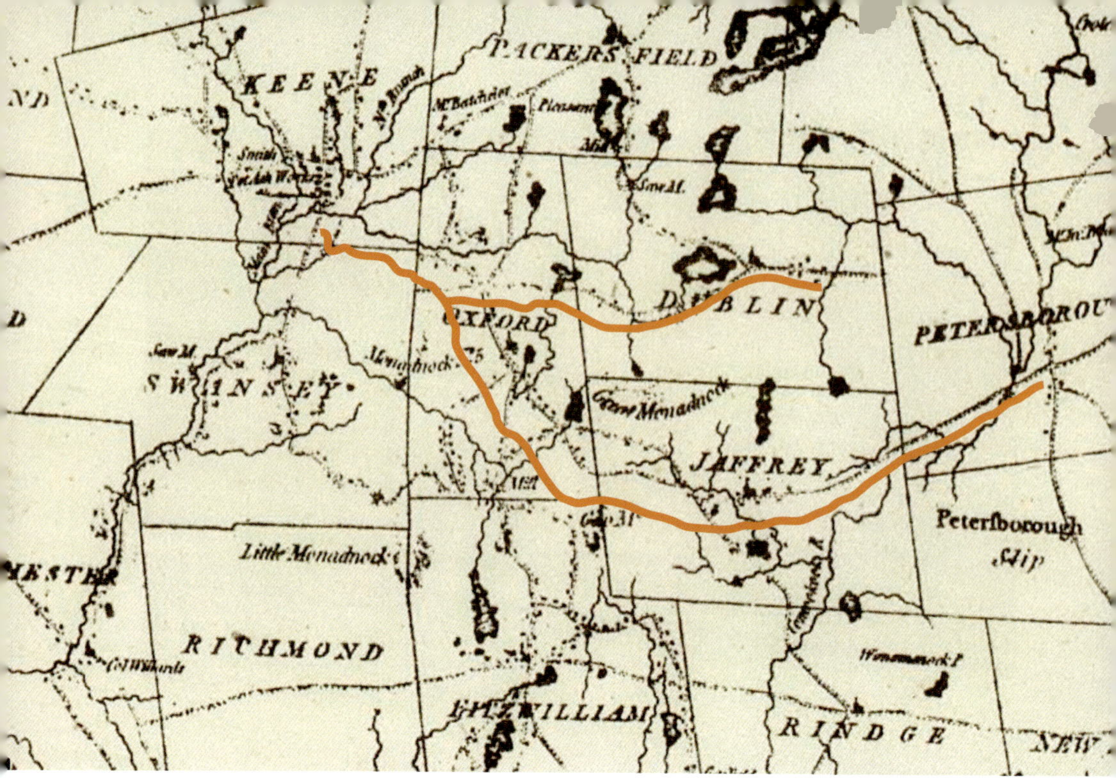

A detail from Holland's Map, which was drawn in 1774 for English knowledge of road use, and appears in Jones, MacClintock's Journey. Marked on it here are military or great roads through Jaffrey and Dublin, yet around Monadnock.

So we are on a branch of the great road, one of many branches, sometimes carrying other names. It is a part of long-route tributaries that flow to other branches, and may have consolidated to become a river of soldiers as it left Keene to the northwest, as shown on Holland's Map of 1774.[26] In 1735 and before, it would have started as simply marked trees penetrating Abenaki country. It remains by far the oldest network of colonial routes of this region, marked out only a decade after those pioneer colonial explorers were entering the wigwams of another people on Monadnock. Neighborhood tradition in Troy supports its presence between the two mountains. At least briefly we are riding the track that some colonial soldiers marched as a military route leading to distant wars.

As if to underscore Kidd's scholarship, our venerable but paved road has a fork; the fork zigs quickly northwest again and becomes gravel Old County Road. It leads us uphill but not over a mountain. Likely, long before there were "county" roads, some of those same tracks existed as part of a military route called a great road. Because the great roads held meaning, the old name sometimes remains.[27]

And before that? It was Abenaki country. It is not so surprising that the very oldest long routes that existed were the ones used for literally thousands of years by the Abenaki and their ancestors, shaped largely by the land. Archeologist Chester Price studied where such trails lay. Travel in this area focused on the canoeing rivers: the Contoocook, the Minnewawa, the Ashuelot crossing to the Connecticut. But river travel included long "secondary" routes over heights of land—around Monadnock.

These long trails are drawn on Price's map. Heading generally west, the first is "Monadenok," crossing Jaffrey into Troy. It looks to be approximately Jaffrey's "Great Road," to quote Jaffrey's sign. The second trail, "Minniwawa," heading generally northwest, passes the mountain approximately at Lake Road, on the south side of Dublin Pond. Below that height, traveling mostly by water to Minnewawa Brook would have made an efficient route to our Marlborough and Keene and the Abenaki's Ashuelot River artery. That is roughly the course of our highway, US Route 101. Price's map, and that of Holland, surveyed in 1774, have some relationship. [28]

Today this narrow gravel way, Old County Road and likely more names, offers us serene beauty once more. Its borders are great beech trees, which filter the view of long hillside fields. Can Misty feel through my body how much I enjoy riding here? People say, Yes. She is moving completely comfortably. At the crest of the hill is another pristine and historic white home, Horizon Hill Farm, settled in 1792, its house and barn rebuilt by generations of one nineteenth-century family, first Stephen Adams, and later Daniel P. Adams, who built the barn. The barn of this farm is said to be the biggest one preserved in the region. As we pass the house, sure enough, an extension of outbuildings rises to a traditional barn, but the barn is huge. It is magnificent—excellently kept yet appearing unpainted. Its windows look small because the barn's size belies its distance from us.[29]

At the end of the lawn, the road seems to vanish. Under foliage, a dirt path draws us into the forest—still Old County Road, and still it aims directly between the slopes of Gap Mountain hidden to our left and the slopes of Monadnock somewhere to our right. It serves the purpose of a great road. Now we are riding in a very soft rain. The drops are scarcely

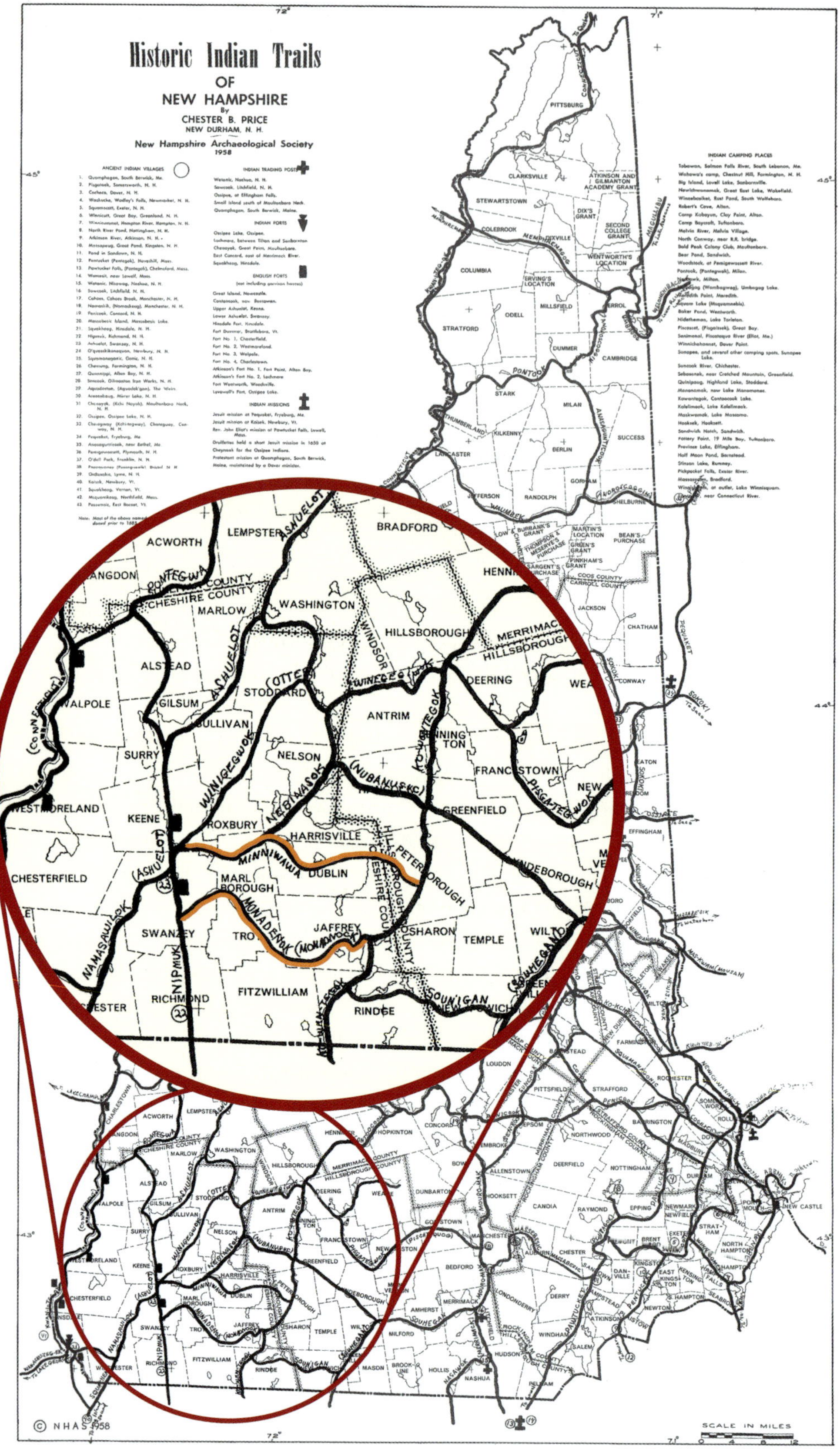

Historic Indian Trails
OF
NEW HAMPSHIRE
By
CHESTER B. PRICE
NEW DURHAM, N. H.
New Hampshire Archaeological Society
1958
ANCIENT INDIAN VILLAGES
1. Quamphegan, South Berwick, Me.
2. Pisgoiook, Somersworth, N. H.
3. Cocheco, Dover, N. H.
4. Washucke, Wadley's Falls, Newmarket, N. H.
5. Squamscott, Exeter, N. H.
6. Winnicutt, Great Bay, Greenland, N. H.
7. Winnicunnet, Hampton River, Hampton, N. H.
8. North River Pond, Nottingham, N. H.
9. Atkinson River, Atkinson, N. H.
10. Massapaug, Great Pond, Kingston, N. H.
11. Pond in Sandown, N. H.
12. Pentucket (Pentegok), Haverhill, Mass.
13. Pawtucket Falls, (Pentegok), Chelmsford, Mass.
14. Wamesit, near Lowell, Mass.
15. Watanic, Nhawag, Nashua, N. H.
16. Sowcook, Litchfield, N. H.
17. Cohoes, Cohoes Brook, Manchester, N. H.
18. Namaskik, (Namaskeug), Manchester, N. H.
19. Penicook, Concord, N. H.
20. Massabesic Island, Massabesic Lake.
21. Squakheag, Hinsdale, N. H.
22. Nipmuk, Richmond, N. H.
23. Ashuelot, Swanzey, N. H.
24. O'quasskikanaquon, Newbury, N. H.
25. Squamanagonic, Gonic, N. H.
26. Chemung, Farmington, N. H.
27. Quinnipgi, Alton Bay, N. H.
28. Suncook, Gilmanton Iron Works, N. H.
29. Aquadoctan, (Aquadok'gan), The Weirs
30. Aceotabaug, Mirror Lake, N. H.
31. Chenayok, (Kchi Noyoh), Moultonboro Neck, N. H.
32. Ossipee, Ossipee Lake, N. H.
33. Chesegway (Kchi-tegway), Chateguay, Conway, N. H.
34. Pequaket, Fryeburg, Me.
35. Anasagunticook, near Bethel, Me.
36. Pemigewassett, Plymouth, N. H.
37. O'dell Park, Franklin, N. H.
38. Pasquaney (Pasing-wealk), Bristol, N. H.
39. Ordanakis, Lyme, N. H.
40. Koisek, Newbury, Vt.
41. Squakheag, Vernon, Vt.
42. Mequamkeag, Northfield, Mass.
43. Passumsic, East Barnet, Vt.
Note: Most of the above named
doned prior to 1685
INDIAN TRADING POSTS
Watanic, Nashua, N. H.
Sowcook, Litchfield, N. H.
Ossipee, at Effingham Falls.
Small island south of Moultonboro Neck.
Quamphegan, South Berwick, Maine.
INDIAN FORTS
Ossipee Lake, Ossipee.
Lochmere, between Tilton and Sanbornton.
Chenayok, Great Point, Moultonboro.
East Concord, east of Merrimack River.
Squakheag, Hinsdale.
ENGLISH FORTS
(not including garrison houses)
Great Island, Newcastle.
Contoocook, now Boscawen.
Upper Ashuelot, Keene.
Lower Ashuelot, Swanzey.
Hinsdale Fort, Hinsdale.
Fort Dummer, Brattleboro, Vt.
Fort No. 1, Chesterfield.
Fort No. 2, Westmoreland.
Fort No. 3, Walpole.
Fort No. 4, Charlestown.
Atkinson's Fort No. 1, Fort Point, Alton Bay.
Atkinson's Fort No. 2, Lochmere
Fort Wentworth, Woodsville.
Lovewell's Fort, Ossipee Lake.
INDIAN MISSIONS
Jesuit mission at Pequaket, Fryeburg, Me.
Jesuit mission at Koisek, Newbury, Vt.
Rev. John Eliot's mission at Pawtucket Falls, Lowell, Mass.
Druillettes held a short Jesuit mission in 1650 at Cheynook for the Ossipee Indians.
Protestant mission at Quamphegan, South Berwick, Maine, maintained by a Dover minister.
INDIAN CAMPING PLACES
Tobawan, Salmon Falls River, South Lebanon, Me.
Wahawa's camp, Chestnut Hill, Farmington, N. H.
Big Island, Lovell Lake, Sanbornville.
Newichwanamak, Great East Lake, Wakefield.
Winnebasiket, Rust Pond, South Wolfeboro.
Robert's Cove, Alton.
Camp Kabayun, Clay Point, Alton.
Camp Baycroft, Tuftonboro.
Melvin River, Melvin Village.
North Conway, near R.R. bridge.
Bald Peak Colony Club, Moultonboro.
Bear Pond, Sandwich.
Woodstock, at Pemigewassett River.
Pontook, (Pontegwak), Milan.
Meredith Point, Meredith.
Baker Pond, Wentworth.
Nidetheman, Lake Tarleton.
Piscasset, (Pisgoiasek), Great Bay.
Senimonal, Piscataqua River (Eliot, Me.)
Winnichahannat, Dover Point.
Sunapee, and several other camping spots, Sunapee Lake.
Suncook River, Chichester.
Sebaseneak, near Crotched Mountain, Greenfield.
Quinipaug, Highland Lake, Stoddard.
Menanomak, now Lake Monomonac.
Kowantegok, Contoocook Lake.
Kalelimook, Lake Kalelimook.
Maskwamak, Lake Mascoma.
Hooksek, Hooksett.
Sandwich Notch, Sandwich.
Pottery Point, 19 Mile Bay, Tuftonboro.
Province Lake, Effingham.
Half Moon Pond, Barnstead.
Stinson Lake, Rumney.
Pickpocket Falls, Exeter River.
Massasecum, Bradford.
near Connecticut River.
PITTSBURG
CLARKSVILLE
STEWARTSTOWN
COLEBROOK
COLUMBIA
STRATFORD
ODELL
MILLSFIELD
DUMMER
ERROL
CAMBRIDGE
STARK
MILAN
KILKENNY
BERLIN
SUCCESS
LANCASTER
JEFFERSON
RANDOLPH
GORHAM
SHELBURNE
JACKSON
CHATHAM
CONWAY
EFFINGHAM
LOUDON
PITTSFIELD
STRAFFORD
ROCHESTER
BARRINGTON
NORTHWOOD
DEERFIELD
NOTTINGHAM
CONCORD
HOPKINTON
ALLENSTOWN
HOOKSETT
DUNBARTON
CANDIA
RAYMOND
EPPING
MANCHESTER
AUBURN
CHESTER
BEDFORD
LONDONDERRY
DERRY
MERRIMACK
AMHERST
MILFORD
HUDSON
WINDHAM
SALEM
NASHUA
HOLLIS
MASON
NEWTON
HAMPTON
NORTH HAMPTON
NEW CASTLE
ACWORTH
LEMPSTER
BRADFORD
LANGDON
CHESHIRE COUNTY
MARLOW
WASHINGTON
HILLSBOROUGH
ALSTEAD
STODDARD
WINDSOR
MERRIMACK
DEERING
WALPOLE
GILSUM
SULLIVAN
ANTRIM
SURRY
NELSON
FRANCESTOWN
WESTMORELAND
KEENE
ROXBURY
HARRISVILLE
GREENFIELD
CHESTERFIELD
MARLBOROUGH
DUBLIN
PETERBOROUGH
SWANZEY
JAFFREY
SHARON
TEMPLE
RICHMOND
FITZWILLIAM
RINDGE
ASHUELOT
WINIGEGWOK
MINNIWAWA
MONADENOK (MONADNOCK)
NIPMUK
NAMASAWILOK
PISCATEGWOK
SOUHEGAN
SOUNIGAN
PONTOOK
NEBWASOK
(NUBANUSKC)
SCALE IN MILES
0 4 8 12
© NHAS 1958

The very large nineteenth-century barn by Daniel Adams at Horizon House, Old County Road, Jaffrey.
[PAM GODIN]

noticeable, and this, we comment, is our shortest day for getting wet. Our cart path is rutted clay, dotted with sprays of fallen birch leaves, and grading up and down. The Metacomet–Monadnock hiking trail briefly joins ours from the south. When I notice the sign and the trail, Misty slows and looks at the opening to it with interest. One of her passions is side trails. On familiar ground, Misty habitually offers, with her ears, with her look, to try a side trail. If I am riding alone I love to experiment with her. In fact, I walked down this trail briefly when I was scouting, and I know it ends quickly for a horse among big boulders. She felt me looking at it. But today, not a chance: we are on a mission. On most of these roads, which are entirely new to Misty, she has not even noticed a side trail. Then again, neither have I.

The land is varying, lower now, opening occasionally to small clearings. In this dusky, wooded, silent place we pass two memorial markers, and I think of two more memorials, appropriate and never to be built. One of these markers is for a casualty of World War II, placed here in a field he loved. A second is dated 2012, carrying only a man's name. The third,

LEFT: A detail enlarged from Price, Historic Indian Trails, covers the same land forms as on the Holland's Map detail and indicates long-preceding trails that relate.

my own imagined candidate, is a historical loss—yet another name connecting the villages of Hancock and Dublin. Elliot Due, of Hancock, was a man of color who farmed with his family in Hancock before the Civil War, and apparently became a social victim of rising local racial tensions in the volatile 1840s. Before long he was recorded as in decline in several ways. He died at age forty-seven on an April night, walking or staggering far from home, in Dublin in a shallow, forested brook.[30]

The fourth memorial that I imagine should be a marker for a category of people who tried to endure. Anyone looking at Colonial New England genealogies quickly perceives that in order to rear the working labor necessary for one of these rugged farms, mothers were expected to bear some ten children. Commonly the mother died young, often quickly replaced by another wife who bore multiple children. Many, many ramifications of living in a community are ordeals that do not reach historical records.

What, then, were recorded eighteenth-century ordeals? According to another historic journal, Rev. Samuel MacClintock's journal, 1760, the building of the military roads, and specifically those between Peterborough and Keene, could be an ordeal of the first order. MacClintock volunteered, as the French and Indian War was ending, to march in an army to consolidate the gains at Fort Ticonderoga. He records first the soldiers axing the trees with many casualties, then the horse teams miring and thus the soldiers "being obliged to lift the wheels a great part of the way," having to "climb up, and then descend, very steep precipices," all the while proceeding as fast as possible because provisions, already short, would be available only at a distant goal. By the time they moved into Vermont, with sickness and accidents high and without provisions for days at a time, soldiers were deserting in ever-increasing numbers. MacClintock does not need to specify, I think, the term "ordeal." Abner Sanger had an ordeal even more emotionally harrowing than the soldiers' ordeal when he was enduring the fact of being an imprisoned Tory trying to care for his brother's family in Keene during the Revolutionary War, hitting bottom by sickness and death of two of his brother's children in August 1777. When Abner was allowed to come home for the family in crisis, the six-year-old apparently died in his arms; the three-year-old, who had died two weeks earlier, was named Abner, after him.[31]

Pam, who is riding "rear guard," calls forward that Beauty has been slowing down uncharacteristically. We look out and Pam checks on Beauty's walking for a few more minutes. It's true, she is hardly moving. Something seems wrong. Everything goes quiet. Then Pam tries a remedy that seems to have no cause: she dismounts, takes off girth, saddle and pad, strokes Beauty. She replaces pad and saddle and girth, without any change but very carefully, and remounts. Amazingly to me we proceed normally, and Beauty is well for the rest of our trip. "She was probably a bit tired," Pam says, leaving the mystery.

Later, talking with a friend, fifth-generation farmer Peter Sawyer, I realize he has lived the answer to this mystery. When the tired draft-horse team simply had to stop on the wood-road, Peter's father would get off the double-runner sled, and throw a single log off the load into the woods. Then he would check over everything, as if, but not, to readjust their harnesses with great flourish, and then start them up anew. They did it, always. A world of knowledge and awareness enhances a horseman's or horsewoman's abilities over the years.

This path on low land is fragrant of earth. An ochre ladder of tree mushrooms climbs on an old trunk like some rubbery forest being. We are close to wetland. The path has threaded through one old intersection and now another: at Bullard Road, we follow a sign marked Old Mill Road. This road is significantly named, and it will soon run into the township of Troy. Now it begins to climb gently along a wide brook: Perkins Brook. The trees become large and old, and we can begin to see far into the woods. Beside us even the fallen branches are logs. Once again during this trip, under the forest canopy the land is giving a subtle opened and tamed feeling—to me one of anticipation.

Then we are in it: a totally empty, extensive, and dramatic mill site. This was the Colburn Mill, a sequence of powerful mills humming for over a century at the dependable outlet of Perkins Pond, in the part of Marlborough that became Troy. We can see steep banks, a lower dam, and a low brook rushing around great boulders. The mill site extends far beyond what we can see from horseback. Close to us was a blacksmithy, the smith's home, a mechanic shop, and a smaller mop stick factory. Some humps suggest cabin foundations for mill workers. Great embankments half hidden across the brook were the main mill and a sheep-washing

Old Mill Road leads us past extensive foundations of the Colburn Mills, Troy. [PAM GODIN]

pool. That far brook bank much later held this place's last phase, the Troy Electric Generator, for the township from the early twentieth century. This place is the setting for a lengthening crowd of people over time.[32]

Like the cascade at Bailey Mills, in a wet season these waterfalls can still roar. We climb slightly past the upper mill pond, which is now mostly a rocky flowing brook bed, and the horses clank over a very sturdy bridge above the brook, and through a traffic stile. We turn out into an open empty area as Mill Road ends at Monadnock Street and the outlet of Perkins Pond, Troy. Even this clearing at the meeting of roads is historic: It used to be called "Frost Corner" and it was the site of yet another tavern. Henry David Thoreau walked—or jogged—past here on this "Monadnock Street," heading for Troy in a hurry on September 7, 1852. He was returning from the summit after an intense, many-mile walk from Peterborough across farms and over Monadnock to catch Troy's three o'clock afternoon train home to Massachusetts.[33]

Across the road we can see a sort of green-foliage funnel of a trail as it narrows, rises, and turns from sight. We take that. It carries us away from the road and the pond, and gently winds upward through trees, passing a cottage or two. We enter one more veil of woodland, still on a rising curve.

Now our trail lies between fences, and as we keep moving we can see that these are paddocks. In the paddocks successively are donkeys, curious; then sheep, easing back; then goats, faintly musk-scented and watching us. Now it is enclosures for knobby geese and for chickens, each to its own. Misty is tensing at these sights and scents, but we are moving steadily along. The views begin to extend: above these paddocks is a broad and high pasture hillside, a hill of sheep. Close to us on a lower hillside is a herd of ponies. Farther back and far above the ponies we can see black and white and brown cattle, distant, looking like scattered marbles slowly moving about on a green height—looking like Switzerland. We are arriving at the top of the hill we have been climbing, and we keep walking steadily into life, scent, and sound. Here is a wide courtyard of outbuildings close to us, and behind those, people walking, working, and minding their business. They wave cordially to us as we pass. Now we can see the gables of white houses clustered around the courtyard. Near at hand someone seems to nod at my palfrey and waves us toward another narrowing passage. We dismount, lead our horses onto a fenced wooden ramp, walking now straight toward and through the doorway of a large, commodious barn.

Climbing to the Inn at East Hill Farm, Troy, when seen as medieval romance:
1) Donkeys, curious

2) A hill of sheep, outbuildings
3) Riding into the courtyard
[PAM GODIN]

Misty beckons to any children, East Hill barn.
[PAM GODIN]

The barn is busy, smells of hay, and has a line of named stalls. Here, people usher our horses directly into three well-stocked box stalls.

We have come to The Inn at East Hill Farm in Troy. Personally, this arrival transports me. I'm an old medievalist, and have just experienced riding out of a long forest trek, passing the outlying settlements and then domestic life, closer and deeper into the stronghold, and finally through a gate into the welcome of a courtyard—a classic scene from medieval romance that I never dreamed I would feel. My friends have to prod me gently about until I can return to what we in fact are doing.

Misty, however, sees all this quite differently. She has seen this kind of barn before: comfortable, with low wooden stall doors made, as she sees it, for children to pet ponies. So Misty becomes mellow and fetching, looking around. Now she begins to combine gobbling up fresh hay with extending her head far over the door and nodding vigorously to the world, sure that she can attract a child who will have treats. One of Pam's photos shows Misty with clearly defined neck, but head and mane a blur of vigorous bobbing, and me beside the stall collapsing in laughter.

We relax at the inn, with art of Ann Sawyer.
[PAM GODIN]

Beauty and Jack are content, which is good, because tall Jack could easily clear his stall door if he wanted to, and Beauty, the fox hunter, knows all about the jumping option. They settle right in to eat. Our easy day between inns has been six miles.

This inn has grown up steadily from an old farm that took some boarders in the nineteenth-century era of cattle drovers. Its original settler's story is romantic indeed: his was one of those first dwellings that at least briefly was a cave. The staff say they could take a person to the site of that cave. The first recorded farm-builder was Silas Fife in 1772. The farm was called an inn as of 1834, later known as "Whitcomb's" to the cattle drovers, for 110 years. For the recent two generations, the farm and its inn has been in the David Adams family, several of whom are on its staff. The farm, offering rare livestock, a very hospitable inn, and lots of ideas, has flourished as a destination for a regular clientele of city families who want a weekend of outdoor activity or a real engagement in farm life.[34]

On this grayish September weeknight, the inn is empty of visitors, except for us. The staff, though, is in full swing—they pour hospitality on

A cottage at East Hill Farm.
[PAM GODIN]

us and we love it. They furnish us with a sturdy cottage that usually holds a family of five. They provide us with a complete and hearty roast-pork dinner in the big post-and-beam dining hall. The chef comes over to greet us and mentions that he has been the chef here for thirty years.

In the evening we relax happily in our new cottage living room, talking, with more champagne and a bit of text-messaging. Shelley has been trying out a video camera on a harness at her chest. So we check out a video stream from our sunny morning on Gilson and Dublin roads in Jaffrey. It features, of course, the rust-red ears and cream and gray arched neck of Jack. On video, his ears and crest gently undulate in a perfect rhythm that could be set to music. Even more gently the whole picture is undulating, all the time. The green scenery is rolling toward us from a point of horizon between the ears, widening to flow rhythmically past on each side. We find this hypnotic rocking world both fascinating and, for us tonight, entirely merry.

DAY THREE

On the Northern Slopes—Marlborough and Dublin

Howe Reservoir
Beech Hill
Hurricane Hill
Dark Pd
Dublin Pond
Sprague Hs
Spaulding Hill
Dolbear ptg, 1860
Stone Pd
Sunset Hill
Dublin Golf Club
Morses' Mill
Scott's Tavern
Sanger Site
J. Allison
Lake Rd
Snow Hill Rd
Old Marlborough Rd
Learned Rd
Puffer
Bixby Hs
Close Rd
D. Gleason
Hoar
Old Troy Rd
Ph. Gleason
Farmers Trail
Farrar
Gleason Bk
Pumpelly Trail
Goodenow
Brook
Marlboro Trail
Monadnock Mtn
Fire Lookout
Gilson Pd
Davis
Mountain Rd
Shaker Farm Rd
White Arrow Trail
White Dot Trail
Red Cross Trail
Cascade Link
Harling Trail
Upper Jaffrey Rd
Gilson Rd
Bigelow Hill
Haskell's Tavern
Halfway House
Gibbs Rd
Perkins Pd
Poole Res
Fassett
Old Keene Rd
Inn at East Hill Farm
Brook
Old Mill Rd
Whites Path
Whites Pd
Milliken Rd
Cummings Meadow
Mead Brook
Gap Mtn
Fern Hill
Old County Rd
Great Rd
Cubleigh Hill
Potters Pd
Fitzwilliam Rd
Jaffrey

Pam returns with photo of earliest
sunlight on Monadnock, East Hill Farm.
[SHELLEY MOZIER]

THURSDAY, SEPTEMBER 29, 2016

This early morning, a thick cloud still looms, but below it we can see the view. We are looking at the lower half of Monadnock directly above Perkins Pond. Slowly the cloud is taking on dawn peach and rose tints—it is beginning to lift. East Hill Farm is another extravagantly beautiful location, and the houses and cottages all share this sight.

First, I go to my pony. Last evening, while I was in my medieval reverie, Pam came over to help me check the lock on Misty's stall door. Pam and I both know that one of Misty's major secrets is that she is a breakout expert. Any time that I am working with a chain or a barrel bolt, Misty is watching me closely and learning. If there is a lock within her reach she will toss it around on its hasp or bolt and play with it until it opens. So in any stall I find a way to double-lock her in. A loose horse may find an unlocked grain-room door, and eat until it founders. A loose Misty in particular always means a barn the next morning in chaos—everything on the floor, pulled off hooks, pulled down from shelves, and tossed about.

Up to this point in time, Misty has digested whatever she may have eaten.

Last night Pam had found me forgetting about this. She had very diplomatically produced a hay string and tied a good knot over the bolt, "just in case." I had quickly doubled that knot, but still: questions are propelling me ever faster toward the barn. I charge in and—all is just as we left it. I greet the tranquil Misty and look hard at the lock. The string is still holding the door closed, but the bolt has been opened.

The staff are still giving us extra attention. (They have no idea what news they have just been spared.) They think to serve us a big breakfast featuring homemade muffins in a cozy side room with a fire in the fireplace. They provide us with bag lunches for the trail.

Our plan for our last morning is to traverse the inn trails north around Perkins Pond until those trails turn us out on Route 124. After less than half a mile on the highway we will leave it for the old and graveled Shaker Farm Road heading northeast. Weeks ago, inn owner Dave Adams advised me that the lightest and safest traffic on the highway occurs in middle morning. So it is that we are tacking up in the barn in a leisurely manner in order to ride out about ten o'clock. A staff member strides into the barn.

"Just want to warn you that one hundred elementary school children are about to come in to ride in a covered wagon down the driveway you are taking."

That does it. We rush, scramble aboard, and parade out into a crowd of children. Just behind the children the covered wagon, already starting to move, halts. We walk the horses in stately fashion through the crowd of children to the driveway out, I, of course, muttering fiercely under my breath to Misty to keep it together. At the last second, I think of my legacy for these children as a happy horseback rider, look up, and wave genially back to them. They respond. We're on our way.

How quickly these worlds change when viewed from horseback. It is quiet again. We are winding through the woods on a lovely ski trail. We come out on the pavement of the commuters' highway, Route 124 and still named The Mountain Road, heading northwest. My friends arrange Misty and me in the middle, single file. Our passage is just fine: none of the few passing vehicles rattles or speeds or even lifts our hairs as the horses walk this narrow margin. Our highway, without fanfare, has passed us into Marlborough township. As we near our goal of Shaker Farm Road, we pass a major landmark. Haskell's Tavern was a teamster's delight from 1803 until 1845. Its ramparts have become a huge mound of rocks extending back from the remaining slight dent in the foliage, a mound pointing toward a filtered view of the mountain over distant houses. Haskell's was a many-storied place. It had the reputation of having the best view and the jolliest scenes within.[35]

The horse story, however, took place at Sweetser's Tavern of eastern Marlborough, just over the hill, in around the 1790s and hosting most of the same characters.

October 2, 1799:

Today was a Muster Day in Jaffrey, a great gathering. Men coming home have crowded into Sweetser's Tavern, where rum has been flowing for hours and the place is alive. Voices suddenly rise. At the bar someone is baiting Henry Hunt, horseman, landowner. Hunt is the man that Phinehas Farrar had to beat out in arbitration. He's the man Abner Sanger had to be talked out of suing for broken agreements, and that talking was not done to save Hunt. Everybody is listening.

"Henry, you have a good colt, but he's not ready yet. He's young, and he's green. He can't climb a hill."

"That colt can climb anywhere."

"I'll wager you can't make him climb the staircase into this hall."

They all know Hunt is full of "spirit." He jumps up now, strikes the bar. He accepts the bet. Chairs scrape, men gather, money flows onto the table. Hunt strides downstairs and out. Talk rises, and so do expectations.

Henry Hunt crashes back through the doorway at the bottom of the stairs. He's got his slender black Dutch horse, about two years old. Everybody is laughing, and then they go quiet, watching. Hunt whistles and whacks, and steps ahead with the lead line. The colt puts a hoof on the first tread. The animal looks calm, even interested. The colt begins to climb, and the hall begins to roar.

In triumph Hunt leads his colt from the top step over to the bar and begins to collect his debt. Applause follows him. Someone offers the horse a sip of toddy. Finally Hunt turns, majestic, money in his pockets, and leads the horse back to the staircase. Right at the top step, the horse stops short. Hunt urges. He steps down and pulls. He whips.

He pushes. The ears are back, the eyes are white: the colt braces. He won't budge. Now the laughter is changing to derision. Hunt keeps working. Everyone can see it: this colt will take anything, but he won't move down.

"So don't just sit there, neighbors, help me out," Hunt growls. "Benjamin. This is your job. Get up here." No one in the hall moves an inch. There is a long pause, silence except for the spaced-out reports of whip on hide, and hard breathing from Hunt. Hunt stops, gives the crowd a look.

"Guess I'll have to kill him, then, to get him out of here." Whack. No one moves. Silence. Hunt and his colt are wet with sweat.

"For the man who can get him all the way down the stairs, I'll sponsor your bet after." Nothing. Long, long stillness.

"Look." His voice softens. "I'll sponsor the whole reckoning on toddies all around, now. And then we'll do it."

"The full bet?"

"The full bet."

The thing is done. Every man gets his full share of toddies and the tavern is noisy again. The scene has returned to normal, except for one black horse in the middle of it all. Everyone satisfied, the crowd stands, gathers, begins to push toward the stairs. The colt stumbles and lurches down the stairway and out. As does, finally, Henry Hunt.[36]

And we, riding in a different horse story, finish this last section of highway and begin the forested dirt-road connections that circle north of the mountain. The narrow Shaker Farm Road is a major turn in our circuit, from the storied freight-route area to the quieter settlers' paths coming up from the south and west.

I guess I am revealing to Misty, in ways I don't even know, how glad I am to be back on this kind of road. She was obedient on the highway, but we are both relaxing now. At first there are houses, but we are just flowing along by them. A young mother and two children come into their yard to call greetings. They keep their distance, seeming to know what works best. She asks if we need water; we thank her but no, and keep moving; she cheers us on.

In this area, no visible network of small roads remains to provide any options for travel. This road seems to have been laid out as a longer

Richard and Lois Davis, cellar hole of ca. 1778 at Marlborough trailhead, Shaker Farm Road, Jaffrey. [JASON HALLIWELL]

connection between the settlements. Only the borders of townships have fluctuated over time, but early neighbors ignored those. Shaker Farm Road will lead us on a large curve heading toward Dublin. It does not go through into Dublin for cars—but it does for horses. For me this is another joy. This is mature woodland, still remote, and the road has kept its feeling of great age. For one example, it looks exactly as I recall on summer outings with my family seventy years ago.

Most of the farmers in this area settled about a decade after their peers had chosen Jaffrey's slopes with the southern exposure. Some of them came north around the mountain on approximately our route; others flowed up from Massachusetts on the Old Marlborough Road that lies ahead of us. A favorite early starting spot for a farm included finding some flat area on the mountain with a brook, and any kind of junction where people might be passing—for safety, for potential market access, and sometimes for sociability.

Apparently, settlers' first habitual climb of the mountain was for blueberries, so there were early trails on the mountain, which would attract crowds by mid-nineteenth century. Each of at least three early Monadnock trailheads once held a house on our route. Halliwell has discovered the first of the three cellar holes when one is traveling Shaker Farm Road from this end: it marks the house of Thomas Barnes, a clergyman from Windham, Connecticut, who was already living there by 1778. The spot is about half a mile ahead on the right, on a small flattish hill below a rising area marked on my USGS map with somewhat forgiving contour lines, "where the old road across the Western mountainside came out."[37] My own focus is on those houses that belonged to people interacting with the neighbor who kept a journal.

The second cellar hole is one of these, about two-tenths of a mile farther along Shaker Farm Road, at the Marlborough trailhead, the map showing township of Jaffrey but with settlers' orientation toward Dublin. The cellar is noticeable to hikers and very striking, built of large, cleanly squared rocks, with an outline of rooms that step down a slope, a carpet of lily-of-the-valley groundcover still vigorous and blooming beside it.

Richard Davis and his wife, Lois Whitney, and their family were living here in 1778 as well, though their deed on the lot, from Thomas Barnes, was dated 1795, when they also bought his house. Chamberlain offers that the Davises may have opened this trail. Richard Davis was a shoemaker, as was one of his four sons—this in an era when poor farmers

An oak lies over Shaker Farm Road.
[SHELLEY MOZIER]

A carriage shed was still beautiful and standing at the Shaker Farm site, Jaffrey, in 2012. [JASON HALLIWELL]

were endlessly repairing their own shoes. The Davis farm stayed in the family until 1846, and was inhabited until 1885. Chamberlain details the layout: "It was a story-and-a-half structure, but being built on the slope its kitchen was on the south side. It is said that dancing parties used to be held in that kitchen."[38]

We slowly ride up the inclined trail, beside the lilies-of-the-valley, toward the parking area. We riders can look into the stepped-down granite rectangles that made this dwelling. The mass of the chimney is built into the bank by the trail. Passing just uphill from the foundation, we can see a stone wall running parallel to the house site, made of massive granite. Horseback is perfect for looking over this site.

Silas Davis, elder son of Richard Davis, was the one who attracted his neighbor Abner Sanger's entries for a time. When young Davis was about twenty-four, Sanger first mentions him in July 1794: "William Upton and Silas Davis goes down to Meeting on three colts." Three weeks later Sanger and Davis were "reaping" together with other men, working in trade on another's farm. But the most frequent journal entries come in the same year when men were preparing for "Light Infantry" gatherings that were social occasions. Sanger's stepdaughter, Betsey Meed, who was

Benjamin and Mary Goodenow, cellar hole of home, 1771. Later they added two barn cellars. Shaker Farm Road, Marlborough.
[JASON HALLIWELL]

a seamstress, aged twenty, became much in demand to make "infantry clothing," and no one visited her or borrowed her services, to make a surtout or other such clothing, more often than Silas Davis.

> Betsey Meed and her mam washes this afternoon. Silas Davis goes to town, calls to have Betsey Meed ready to go up with him to tailor a surtout. He comes along near sundown; Betsey goes.[39]

To me the implied privilege showing in Sanger's first journal entry on Davis and the social nature showing in his later ones suggest that life for Silas Davis was significantly easier than it was for Sanger. I like to think that Davis' taste in style relates to those dancing parties.

The morning is sunny, the temperature perfect, the horses comfortable. Since we left the Davises' place at the Marlborough trailhead our road has become a "wood-road" trail, furrowed and rougher, but it carries us right on. A great gnarled oak has fallen above our path, but not low enough to block our passage under it. In a relatively level lowland we cross a small bridge over one of the mountain's most remote brooks, Mountain Brook. Again we let the horses drink briefly from a puddle.

We come to a historic marker, and I am so intent on getting us to the oldest sites that I forego this turn. But this spot once held a notable pioneer, before the road was named. This is the land the Society of Protestant Christians, called Shakers, from Shirley, Massachusetts, chose for their colony beginning in 1810, continuing there until 1883. They accumulated some six hundred acres in Jaffrey, Marlborough, and Dublin, which included a stock farm. To establish their colony on this road, ultimately they had to buy out two settlers.

The second of these settlers' homes became the Shakers' residential house. According to the *History of Marlborough*, that home was built by Benjamin Goodenow, a brave pioneer in 1771—the first permanent settler who had ventured to homestead north of Monadnock.[40] It was he that Abner Sanger noted in his journal on one searing July day in Keene, 1780.

> Merchant Benjamin Goodenow's teams come up with salt and rum from Sudbury. The teamsters severe hot in afternoon.

Benjamin Goodenow came from a Marlborough, Massachusetts, family, born in 1747. He and his wife, Mary, raised a big family here. According to the Marlborough history, after 1794 Goodenow and Benjamin Dole shared with four others a humorous title suggestive of the ancient Israelites on account of their large families.[41] One of the records shows this merchant repeatedly driving freight teams between the Boston area and the Keene area and north. Halliwell's photographs show a strong, squared cellar hole surrounding a big rock chimney foundation—and the front doorstep still in place. The very large outline of the greater barn suggests to me that Goodenow sometimes kept his teams at home; but possibly, such a large barn would have been built by and for the Shaker colony.

Goodenow had also fought at Ticonderoga, and there he contracted a long "slow intermitting fever." His army discharge papers carry a brief description of him by Colonel Isaac Wyman of Keene.

The summit dominates the open knoll of Phinehas and
Lovina Farrar's farm site of 1788, Old Troy Road, Marlborough.
[FRANCELIA CLARK]

> I recommend Benjamin Goodenow . . . under my command, aged twenty-nine years, about five feet eight inches high, dark brown hair, blue eyes, dark complexion, belonging to the town of New Marlborough in New Hampshire, New England, as a proper person to be discharged . . .

A reader can see physically for a moment the man who lived here—respected soldier, earliest settler, merchant, long-distance teamster, who was also farming and rearing a big family. Goodenow died at age seventy-eight in 1825. His farm was bought by the Shakers in 1839, lasting until 1883.

Our wood-road descends roughly, then becomes graded gravel. In deep woods Shaker Farm Road ends at a T-intersection with Old Troy, or Old Dublin, Road. The intersection includes Gleason Brook, mossy and small in this season but flowing well. Again I planned (in this case, very quietly pruned) a hidden drinking spot for the horses here, but again they are just fine to keep going. We turn right, heading toward the area of the Dublin farmers on the northern slopes.

Just after our turn onto Old Troy Road, at Marlborough's border with Dublin, the land opens to a large pastured hill with a grassy driveway heading up. This is my goal for a lunch spot, and my candidate for most beautiful farm site—the farm of Phinehas Farrar, a major citizen of Marlborough. The land became the first settlement in the township of Marlborough when pioneer Isaac McAlister cleared and built a log cabin on it for himself and wife and four children by 1764. Using Continental currency, which became devalued, McAlister could not afford to keep this farm, and moved on. Phinehas Farrar, a sixth-generation American colonist, born in Sudbury, Massachusetts, in 1747, had bought lots in the area as early as 1768, and bought this farm in 1788. He and his wife, Lovina Warren, reared ten sons and a daughter on the farm, and the farm stayed in their family until 1861.[42]

Phinehas Farrar first drew a journal entry from Abner Sanger on that affair wherein Henry Hunt apparently had cheated one of Farrar's sons:

> John Rollins has to go to Esquire Farrar's in Marlborough to stop an action sold by Henry Hunt to young Farrar.

This appears to refer to the process of arbitration, a frequently successful method of drawing trusted and dependable people together to settle a dispute. There were distant courts, and Farrar was a member of one, but the local and frequent arbitrations seem to have been a valuable asset to community life. Farrar was a steady member of such arbitrations and a selectman, as well as Marlborough's representative to the General Court at Concord.

Farrar was a horseman. Sanger mentioned him again as part of a quick picture on an October evening of three citizens seen working together:

> After sundown Esquire Farrar of Marlborough and Captain Hoar of Dublin are jockeying in cattle with Rev. Mr. Sprague.[43]

The *History of Marlborough* is more obviously revealing, calling Farrar "Esquire" and "Captain" and "Doctor," and including a sprightly list of his charges in 1789, apparently when he was a new resident, "for servis as committee to finish building the meeting house." According to this hint, and to his own list, Farrar may have been the entire committee. His charges include:

At the Farrar farm site, a walled cow path heads down slope, and on this day, the family well gives a view of the author looking in.
[FRANCELIA CLARK]

> To half a Day Settling with the old Committee
> To two journeys to John Parkhurst after Nails
> To five time attending vandue to Sel the Pues
> And once to Keene after Iron
> To cuting and Drawing stage Poles
> To Carting one load of Plunk
> Once to Warrins after Rumb for the carpenters
> To one journey to Fitzwilliam after Nails
> To time spent after stuf
> To my Cart to Dublin after a barril of Rumb
> To three half days settling with people
> To Cash Paid for glew
> To me and horse, one Day after Calves pates

This is less than half his list.[44]

The Marlborough history's proudest record of Phinehas Farrar is from several years later, by Phillips Sweetser, of Sweetser's Tavern. Sweetser recommended that Town Meeting re-elect Farrar as representative to Concord despite his already long service there:

> "Let me give you a few words of advice. If you want a man to represent you in the General Court of this state, send Esquire Farrar by all means, for he has been so many times he knows the way, and the necessary steps to be taken."[45]

Farrar's farm site is expansive, still holding high and long fields on a knoll opposite the summit. From Halliwell's correspondence I know that the site still shows evidence of stone enclosures, a stone-walled cow road down to the pasture, a well near the cellar hole and a well for the cows—a veritable anatomy of a farm site. But when we arrive with horses at the grass driveway up to the hill site, despite my best planning it is blocked. There is a new gate and tight fence, and we cannot justify trying to enter. So today we must pass it by.

Weeks later I reached one of the present owners of Farrar's farm, who graciously hosted Shelley and me on a walk within the site. The retired owner, who worked the farmland but always lived nearby, grew up in a very traditional farm family that has owned this land since just after the Civil War. She taught me a lot about what we were seeing. On that bright December day, she stepped into the cellar hole to show its depth. Near

At Phineas and Hannah Rowell Gleason's cellar hole of 1784 on Old Troy Road, Dublin, horses can still move about. The pond is in the background.
[PAM GODIN]

that, she lifted a wire lid to reveal the well water deep below. The circle of water reflected our peering heads.

The owner could not resist a laugh that day when I tried out my new "aesthetics theory" of a settler choosing a farm site for its beauty. "No," she said. "It's all about exposure—a southern exposure and a lot of open space to let the sunlight in." Of course, I realized: a lot of open space at Monadnock means inherently a beautiful view. Only then I noticed that this knoll on the north side of the mountain actually has much southern exposure. She said that the soil is in fact good, containing important nutrients, "If there's enough of it."[46] They had raised cattle and chickens, sometimes pigs, and kept their hayfields yielding up until recent years. She cherished her days growing up on this land, sledding, gathering eggs, churning butter, hosting a pig roast, listening to her father's stories. She has also had a significant professional career. In an important sense, she has never left, and never wants to leave, her beloved place. Given how much the American culture has necessitated change, she is a farmer who stayed.

From all we have learned, "Esquire" Phinehas Farrar registers as a person of ethics, energy, spirit, and major contribution to his broader community. He drew wide trust from people and used it well. He in fact was a solver of his community's ordeals. And he did very well when he chose this farm.

We have come into the township of Dublin on Old Troy Road. Our old gravel road carries us in deep woods. I am looking toward the mountain slope for a flattened, low hill just over the stone wall. The woods are of medium age, with that subtle once-cared-for look of use. Here's the gap in the wall, above the road bed, and the horses were not expecting this one. I slow down and give a distinct right rein to the ever-curious Misty, and she gamely climbs the bank. The others follow readily.

An upward slant leads us into the woods, no trail. But the woods mysteriously stand open enough to let horses pass. In fact, it was once a trail, the short farm road up to another pioneer's site, that of Phineas Gleason. After several yards rising gently, the land opens out, still under the tree canopy. On the left are irregular clumps of rock. On the right is the shallow stone-wall outline of a barn or paddock. Ahead is a depression holding a small, dark pond. The area is so open under the canopy that the horses can move about here and let us explore. Pam spreads out a bit and rides over to look at the pond. Shelley and I are trying to see these half-buried rocks as parts of an irregular house site. We begin to see that the cellar hole of the house has aged into a narrow, L-shaped crevice between two mature trees.

To me, Phineas Gleason's place feels shadowed because he built one barn into a bank beside that small dark pond. He probably created that low area as a farm pond, because a thin brook runs through its basin, but over great time it has nearly disappeared into a rich black turf, with trees and a slip of open water. Maps faithfully show the pond. Halliwell has identified two wells here, and the walls of a cow path coming down into the barnyard from the higher slopes beyond us. This ghost of a barnyard allows us to keep looking by horseback for trails, looking for the perimeter of the rock outline beside us. A paper-thin rim from an iron wagon wheel lies propped against a tree.

The *History of Dublin* names Phineas Gleason as the first settler in Dublin on the north slope of the mountain, in 1784, "well acquainted with the hardships and privations to which the first settlers were exposed." (We believe he had Marlborough neighbors further down these roads sharing

Daniel and Hannah Rollins Gleason, cellar hole of ca. 1786, at the original Dublin trailhead, Old Troy Road. View is across the big chimney mass, lengthwise along house front. Below is the same house, from nearly the same angle, where Darling's herd grazed in the 1840s and presumably Farmer's herd grazed in 1889.
[JASON HALLIWELL; PHOTO BY J. A. FRENCH, DUBLIN HISTORICAL SOCIETY]

these hardships.) Gleason was born in Sudbury, Massachusetts, in 1757, fought in the Revolution for a year, married Hannah Rowell, who would bear him twelve children, came to Dublin, and bought two lots adjacent to one another. For a time, he and two brothers lived as neighbors spaced out along the Old Troy Road. They are honored by a namesake, Gleason Brook, which pours from above but runs parallel to the road and levels out just beyond this little hill. That is the mossy brook we met back at the intersection where I thought the horses might drink. Two of Gleason's sons inherited this farm in sequence, and the house was last standing to be sold in 1897; it burned in about 1914. The land was kept as pasture until 1953.

As for Phineas Gleason's hardiness, Abner Sanger notes that only Gleason and three other men made it to a "school meeting" in November 1793 on a "very cold, blustery night." Hardiness seems to be a major factor in February 1794, when Gleason and his wife and Jonathan Hoar and his wife go off on a horseback journey together to Marlborough, and from there the first three continue back to Sudbury, Massachusetts. It seems they made it. Most often Gleason seems to have been called upon for his judgment as an arbitrator of neighbors' disputes.

Apparently Phineas Gleason made his greatest contribution in children and education. He was active in schooling decisions. He married off five daughters, and his two surviving sons became "prominent citizens." When he learned that Sanger's stepson, thirteen-year-old David Meed, was losing ambition and spirit for education, he and Jonathan Hoar stepped forward to join Sanger as the boy's legal guardians. With that support, young Meed became an apprentice, then a cordwainer, married, and worked in Massachusetts with his family. The Historical Society of Cheshire County keeps a fine leather pair of women's embroidered slippers made by David Meed. His guardians in hardships realized he was cut out for something else, not conventional schooling and farming.[47]

The forest road becomes wider gravel again. We pass by clearings and trail signs. Soon we are at the parking lot for the Dublin Trail to the summit. This means I have missed a trailhead cellar hole, perhaps because the Dublin trailhead has been moved in recent years. It was Phineas Gleason's brother Daniel Gleason who bought the site from him and built and settled about 1786. Halliwell has pointed out that Daniel Gleason's cellar hole, another impressively large one surrounding a central chimney and lying beside the original trailhead, is itself surrounded by a rectangular perimeter stone wall. I remember it as a place marked by a carpet of vinca, and these are flourishing still. On this day the parking lot is quiet, showing only a few parked cars through a fringe of trees.

Here comes a family with a dog on a long leash, chatting and walking toward us. I have a reason for my intense focus on Misty at such a casual meeting. When I bought her, she was unfazed by people with leashed dogs. But under my nervous tutelage she has begun to lose her cool and try to turn back and exit the scene. Shelley perceived this transformation some weeks ago, and I have been working on it. So I focus hard on both calmness (I hope) and insistence, muttering "Right on through, Misty." She does it. As so often, I look up and smile at these people at the very last second, to their amusement.

Across time Daniel Gleason's farm has gathered other names as a busy trailhead: it is known as the Darling/Farmer/Dublin trailhead. Both Luther Darling and William Farmer had farms near it; both oversaw the trail in their day. Apparently, Luther Darling, who lived in the Daniel Gleason house, used the trail to the summit, probably blazed since the fire of 1820 and lying partially over pastures. Thought of the burned-over pasture reminds me once again of blueberry bushes. It was clearly a place of cows. Darling was climbing to the summit to make flares by the time of a Bunker Hill celebration in 1843, and by 1851 his son Josiah was regularly hosting trail-climbers at the house.

Then, William Farmer's daughter, Genevieve Farmer, was also a notable trail guide for some twenty years. She impressed those who walked up the mountain with her character, her reading, and her knowledge of nature. Thomas Wentworth Higginson commemorated her in a poem of 1902. The house went on hosting before the Civil War, was abandoned in 1902, and was standing until 1916.

Already when it belonged to Daniel Gleason the farm was a place of activity and social life. Dublin settlers often stopped at Abner Sanger's farm on the way to Daniel Gleason's—especially John Rollins, who bartered with Sanger and was the father of Daniel's wife, Hannah Rollins Gleason. Daniel Gleason was thirty-two in 1794. One day he and his wife would follow the Rollins clan off to farm in Vermont.[48]

As for settlers' meetings on the road in daily life, first, I imagine Sanger

From Daniel Gleason's cellar hole, one can imagine the family's view of the summit.
[FRANCELIA CLARK]

on a snowy January day driving a borrowed cow down this road into Daniel Gleason's keeping. Then, I try to imagine Sanger walking home from Gleason's, carrying his own wife's "weaving sley and said Gleason's wife's harness to weave with." This was on March 26, 1794, and if time travel and melting snow had allowed us to be riding horses out here, and if the loom reeds and harness parts were large, for a big loom, I suppose we would have needed to give way. But then, once more I realize how much I do not know, this time about experience for eighteenth-century working horses. They continually hauled or saw everything settlers made or met. Ours are to me remarkable, but the best of those must have been masters of the unexpected.

Jonathan Hoar, cellar hole of 1787, Old Troy Road. The view is of the length of his cellar hole, looking toward the maple. [JASON HALLIWELL]

Through these woods, as we keep riding, the sun is casting striped shadows on the gravel of Old Troy Road. A sign, "no trespassing," though a small one, marks our next cellar hole, and we have come to the spot where this narrative started, the land of Captain Jonathan Hoar. The third brother of the Gleasons, Nathan, bought this lot from a Masonian Proprietor in 1787, and built the house. Jonathan Hoar owned the lot south of the road, had married the Gleasons' sister Lucy in 1783, and apparently moved into this house, though not having a deed until after 1800. Hoar's early dates, except for his military service, are elusive, but his last years were recorded and most productive. In 1795 he proved himself a master carpenter as well as a blacksmith. He built the school house in the middle of Dublin, and "exceeded his obligation," earning a cash bonus "for doing more than his bond obliged him to do." His second marriage was to Betsey Mason in 1807, and they had three more children before he died in 1813. His community valued him: he was frequently chosen for arbitration of disputes, and held a prominent pew in the church. This evidence suggests that Hoar was outreaching and very competent, a broadly appreciated man.[49]

Jonathan Hoar's home site foundation of about 1787 shows strong, thick, and squared granite signs that the house was very large and well built. It was of an imposing two-story, hall-and-parlor style, with central chimney and staircase. His son John, who worked with him, inherited the farm and the beautiful house, and later moved on; the house is traceable through 1853. The size of the sugar maple beyond the chimney ruin seems to suggest how long the place has been a cellar hole.[50]

Clearly, Jonathan Hoar was a close friend of Abner Sanger during the four years that Sanger covered in his journal as a Dublin farmer. This friendship deserves one's focus here. Living half a mile apart, the two frequently stopped at each other's homes. Sanger was an unusual settler in several ways, some of which can be seen in his relations with Hoar. At the same time, Sanger's endless work and friendly connections seem to show him as a representative settler—valuable for learning more about settlers' lives.

What were characteristic interactions between the two farmers? Some of Hoar's visits to Sanger ("We talked") seem to be counseling visits, which were surely needed. Sanger was poor with money, poor with financial matters, shaky with debts and credits. This fact is undoubtedly why he carefully kept a journal of all transactions for twenty years.

Many transactions flowed between Hoar and Sanger, and many of these were about horses. For Sanger, these were horses for the winter, for riding with a pack to a more distant mill, for sledding his children to school, for syrup gathering, and "to see if I want to keep her." Though Sanger was a rider, and his journal records that most of these horses were to some degree lame, they still proved useful for his distinct needs. More generally, it is impossible to tell from the cryptic journal to what extent Hoar was sometimes being tolerant in Sanger's ever-difficult transactions. Sanger did get cheated, and when that happened he seemed to trust no one. Sanger then would tell his journal that he suspected many a weight to be faulty, many a measure to include chaff, even those of Hoar. Under the circumstances, Hoar's comment to Sanger on that cold walk in the sleet, that he could get him a horse for winter, reads for me as a hope, a try. But later when Hoar could not, or did not, get the horse, Sanger recorded this bitterly in his journal as a broken promise. It is the arbitration meetings that show that some people took advantage of the struggling Sanger, and that sometimes both antagonists in an arbitration were at fault. So these two men had successful transactions, and failed transactions, and often for the reader, puzzles of balance.[51]

> February 19, 1794. I send David Meed to Captain Hoar's for a basket of rye. He returns without.
> February 21. Terrible blustering. I go to Captain Hoar's for rye and go to Deacon Morse's to mill. Captain Jonathan Hoar, creditor for one bushel of rye.

Somehow the rye changed hands. Sanger's futile requests of Hoar often transformed on a second try, and in either case the personal relationship seemed to stay cordial.

Then, Jonathan Hoar supported Abner Sanger personally, sometimes in very important ways. Below, I think I see a bridge collapse in a freshet.

> March 18, 1794 [a thaw]. Captain Hoar gets into the water trying to cross over my bridge as he is going to the mill. He returns home without going to the adjourned town meeting or to mill either.
> March 26. I clean up my barn floor and all, set things in good order. Then I go to Captain Hoar and see him. He is sick in bed.
> March 30. Captain Hoar has been better but grows worse. Dr. Maynard sent for.

Between the dates of these excerpts about Hoar's sudden declining health, whose chilling cause I think I know, Sanger was undergoing a continuing, major dispute with his neighbor, Walter Wheeler, also from Keene, who lived across the road. The dispute would later be known as "the hay wars," and in ten days would lead to violence, lawsuits, several arbitrations, a trial, and brief jail term for Wheeler. Accordingly, before Hoar became really sick,

> March 22. Captain Hoar come into my barn, stays some time.
> He talks with Benjamin W. Learned . . .

Learned was well known and respected, an arbitrator. Hoar appears to have interceded to find arbitration on behalf of his friend. There seem to be themes of continuity here. People disputed; they might cheat if they could get away with it; they might fight. But they also tolerated, or else worked out ways to arbitrate, to keep the community going, to make it more stable. The arbitration system most often deflected the ultimate legal system. The local ways of stabilizing appeared in varying forms: in Jaffrey, with the minister's house lot and John Grout; in Marlborough, with people finally going after Henry Hunt's prevarications; and in this Dublin community, where Wheeler, as well as undergoing legal sanctions, was socially forced to move back to Keene and all became tolerable again. Meanwhile, strikingly unselfish acts appeared: here, when Hoar and Gleason joined Sanger in guardianship for David Meed; in Hoar's counseling and seeking arbitration on his friend's behalf; and apparently in Hoar's tolerance when Sanger's bridge failed, when he knew that Sanger was struggling and would fix it "later," which Sanger in fact did. These are powerful bonds among people.

We have ridden a couple of miles since my dream of a picnic at the Farrars' farm, and we are beginning to grow hungry. First, however, we are entering the present again, at a large and beautiful farm. We pass white wooden gates: this is a horse farm. I know nothing about it but its beauty—whole fenced hillsides of grass in sunshine on both sides of the road, and several spaced white gates marking probably hundreds of acres. We ride past its focal point, a low barn with two representative white horses, who seem well trained to be admired but not excitable.

Just beyond the main house, there was a settler's dwelling in 1794. The settler's name was Paul Morse. Abner Sanger mentioned him on two summer days, carrying grass and carrying hay, and on an October day, carrying rye. Apparently Paul Morse farmed this same land. His house was still lived in after 1874. So we are passing old farmland, opened before 1794, which still, or once more, exists on Old Troy Road, and it has greatly expanded.[52]

Benjamin and Phebe Mason, small cellar hole of 1783, above Old Troy Road. This site is steadily disappearing. [JASON HALLIWELL]

As we pass the last white gate of the horse farm, which is open, a logging road disappears into the woods. There is one cellar hole that I will not ask us to explore, but I want to note it for my friends as we pass on the road. The farm owner graciously gave me permission to scout it recently, along with Jason Halliwell, who knows what he is looking at. I tell Pam and Shelley that, just incidentally, this path leads up to the cellar hole of my ancestor, one of three Benjamin Masons. This one was the son of the first Benjamin Mason who moved up about 1765 from Sherborn, Massachusetts, and who was an earliest and active Dublin road builder and carpenter. The son Benjamin was born in 1760 and brought from Sherborn as a small child. At age sixteen he was a fifer at the Battle of Bennington; he became a cooper, married Phebe Norcross in 1783, and settled in Dublin in the same year. The Dublin Map of 1906 Index cites the house on the north mountainside, and the Historical Society's Thaddeus Mason papers of autumn 1782 show Benjamin's older brother Thaddeus bringing in rocks, lumber, clapboards, and shingles to help him build. Benjamin was another surprise from my readings for this trip: I had no idea there was a Mason family up on the mountain. The couple chose to settle high on the north side—facing northeast at about 1,700 feet in elevation as the mountain begins to rise seriously. Most attractive to my imagination, Benjamin is said to have been a wolf hunter.

To get up there, with permission, first one climbs a quarter- to half-mile rise. Then the logging road turns right and the trail stays straight, passing through a lovely small ravine where oak trees surround a very small brook bed. Clambering up the far bank of this ravine when the path begins to turn away from the summit, one can stand up in a small level area—and there it is, a very small cellar hole nearly obliterated by a fallen tree. On this high mountain farm, Benjamin and Phebe Mason successfully reared thirteen out of their fourteen children. None of those took the farm. Nobody ever took it.

Benjamin Mason, one August day when he was thirty-four, met Abner Sanger—when both, probably, were walking on Old Troy Road. This became a note in the journal.[53]

> I agree with Benjamin Mason that he may cut out the road that I hurricaned[54] as I go to Captain Hoar's and put up a handy pair of bars.

In 1852 for Dublin's Centennial celebration, an elder, Ebenezer Morse, remembered his childhood relationship with Benjamin in a poem about Monadnock.

> In these tangled forests the wolves used to roam,
> And howl through the woods when their whelps were half grown;
> And well I remember when my Uncle Ben
> Brought three home alive, which he took from their den.[55]

It's true. He was a wolf hunter.

Could this warm little scene suggest that the fear of wolves among many settlers in this area has been overrated? Or was that fear subconsciously present for people? I try to imagine each moment of the story that historian Alan Rumrill has collected from the earliest history of settlement in Croydon.[56] It takes place near the Sugar River, several miles north of here, but the wolves are the same. We twentieth-century children thought we were told a fairy tale. First, local histories agree that some of the pioneers' first shelters were built with a smoke hole instead of a chimney.

Sugar River, 1770s.

A young mother, Mrs. Benjamin Cutting, walks toward her neighbor's cabin to ask for food. Her husband is away, to meet this same need: their garden is too recent and sparse to sustain the family for winter. He traveled out to get provisions and should get home tomorrow. But today the food has run out. She has not eaten, nor have her children.

The neighbor's homestead is already in her sight. A high sound rises like a horn in the distance. It breaks up into shrill wails. She knows it is wolves. The howls are coming closer, coming on: the neighbors may be here, but her children are at home. She breaks for home at a dead run. She is pounding, not looking back, the yelping is louder and closer. She knows she may not make it.

She lunges through her doorway, slams and bolts it just as the wolves reach the other side. She hugs the small children close, all three at once.

In a few minutes she hears a thudding and scratching against the walls: the wolves are trying to climb to the roof. Then the sound becomes a scuffling overhead. They are treading on the rough bark roof and closing in on the smoke hole. The fire is down to coals.

Her husband took the gun with him. She begins the only possible thing:

"Jacob. Now be like your father and fetch me a stick for the fire."

The child goes to the pile, and the mother seizes the poker and begins to stir up the coals. She makes the sparks and smoke fly. The howling is all coming down through the smoke hole now. Both little boys are running over with logs, and she is stirring madly. Little Abby is bringing kindling—the children are not crying, they are helping. The fire blazes. Log by log, she is keeping the wolves back—and using up the woodpile.

"Daniel, can you bring over that stool? And then fetch another."

A loud cracking and splintering starts overhead. The wolves are trying to bite through the roof, and now the howling is mingling with screams from the children. A shaggy wolf's head appears over the edge

Eli and James Allison's homestead with open mountain view. They were son and grandson of Andrew Allison the early teacher. James was father of Henry D. Allison, who published this photo in Dublin Days, 1952. Old Troy Road lies beyond the house from this viewpoint. [DUBLIN HISTORICAL SOCIETY]

of the hole above. She charges the red-hot poker upward, right at the eye. There is a yelp and the head draws back.

All through the night she goes on, one by one through the furniture and the storage. She's much more frugal with the wood now, but she keeps stirring, keeps the poker in blazing heat. Another wolf's head nudges in above, another charge upward with the poker, and a wail. And another.

Now the family is using up the great bed. The children are running back and forth to the fireside with handfuls from the straw mattress. Even the straw is running low. Gradually they realize there is no longer sound coming from the smoke hole. All has become quiet in the dawn.

The family lived.

There are several regional stories like this. Fairy tales generate from legitimate, thus lingering, fears.

We have been trotting on the even gravel of Old Troy Road, and now, close to its meeting with the Old Marlborough Road, we are passing along in a neighborhood of modern but not new homes, with mature landscaping hiding them and revealing the beginnings of a view ahead. A landscaped gravel driveway to our left marks one more reason for us to pull up. Turning a few feet into the driveway, we can see a barn cellar hole. It is easy to see from horseback, cleaned out and very well cared for, a low and hollow rectangle of granite wall. It marks the home area of Eli Allison, a son of one of Abner Sanger's most valuable benefactors: Andrew Allison, the man who worked hardest to start and keep a neighborhood school for the settlers.[57] Sanger essentially moved heaven and earth to get his children to Allison's school, walking with them in winter, sending Betsey on a horse if that's how she would go, carrying the small ones if necessary—and his children markedly succeeded in their adult lives. The Allison family, including Eli's son who also lived here, James Allison, were a line of descendants who were teachers or school administrators in Dublin and the area. Evidently, they were making a difference.

The Allisons' small barn cellar hole on the homestead, Old Troy Road. Visible beside a well-kept driveway, this now-forested site is hidden in the preceding photo by the main structures. This cellar hole now represents the homestead. [JASON HALLIWELL]

Exploring Abner Sanger's farm site on open land that views the mountain, a working farm after 1762, and Sanger's home from 1790 to 1799. Old Marlborough Road, Dublin.
[PAM GODIN]

Ahead of us we see a change of centuries. Old Marlborough Road lies in front of us in pavement, and across it is the groomed open land of the Dublin golf course. Old Marlborough Road will lead us east around the pond as Lake Road, toward the village of Dublin, and before long to the end of our trip. But all is still very quiet and this land is offering plenty to learn. This section on the south side of Dublin Pond is the ancient trail and road that led to the Ashuelot River, and in another era, to Keene. In Sanger's time it was a storied road, or "highway," as editor Lois Stabler calls it. At that time it came past the historic tavern on the south side of Dublin Pond and led to Marlborough, and from there connected to Keene, and even to Fort Ticonderoga. As it enters Marlborough township this old road passes Stone Pond, as did the military route shown on the Holland map surveyed in 1774. By 1805 a map in the Dublin Historical Society named it County Road. So we turn west on Old Marlborough Road, and we have come onto a great road.

This "highway" is one of the reasons that Abner Sanger moved here. He chose to live on highways, where people were passing by with news. Next to family, his sociability was his vital outlet, and the highway was an artery. As our representative farmer, preceding our own social connections by two centuries, Sanger kept an eye-opening breadth of acquaintances. Among the hundreds of them in Keene, he well knew Colonel Isaac Wyman, who was his own Revolutionary War leader as well as patron in work and the tavern keeper, and Nathan Blake, who had impressed the Abenaki over the two years of his captivity with them. He knew personally Samuel Morison, among the first settlers born in Peterborough; Henry Coffin, many-talented speculator of Jaffrey and Acworth; Breed Batchelder of Nelson, the Tory who took refuge in a cave; Eleazer Wilcox of Gilsum, who wrestled for his life with a bear; and John Kilburn, who lived up to his name at Fort No. 4. He listened to most of the traveling preachers. For any one of these people, he might have a devastating nickname. His twentieth-century editor Lois Stabler counts them all: he names a thousand people.[58]

We are in Sanger's close neighborhood, and coming onto his farm. Finishing Old Troy Road we crossed "his" brook that could flood out a bridge—as Jonathan Hoar learned. This was responsibility. Sanger, son of an intermediary, local-level Proprietor, was somehow educated enough to be a voracious reader of significant books and to write letters for people, but he had long preferred only to help others on their farms with his hard work. He had sold his inherited farm in Keene, and only took charge of this Dublin farm when his older sister Rhoda offered that he live on her one-hundred-acre farm in an exchange of dwellings. Her farm was already long established, and the earliest one we have seen yet, settled on the highway by Levi Partridge in 1762. When Abner Sanger took over this farm in 1790, he was fifty-one years old, having survived a major life watershed in Keene. He had become a Tory in Keene—not a very conducive environment. After tensions (and brief imprisonment) his residence in Keene had continued. But there was a motivation for his move to a Dublin farm: After years of hoping to marry, he had married Elizabeth Johnson Meed, a widow with three children, and was more than ready to support them with his characteristic, continual work.

So to find the land that was written about by this settler, we riders have

On Abner Sanger's farm site—grazing and beyond.
[PAM GODIN]

come onto Old Marlborough Road, deeply sloping down. We cross over the second one of Sanger's bridges, and rise on a long narrow slope above the wetland of "his" brook, Mountain Brook. And here is his central farm site, just beyond the junction of Old Marlborough and Charcoal roads, where many people would be passing. This narrow strip of higher land has now been reopened into a long, lush pastureland. Our Dublin elevation is high, the day has become gloriously clear, and the view south to Monadnock's summit is stunning. Judging by the large amount of clearing on the sloping land, this view must be close to what it was in the 1790s. Sanger's cellar hole is long since filled in, but it is indicated by a slight rise in the field under a flatter grassed area of about the right size. It is near us, and of course near the road, and on the slope, keeping the fullest view.

We have permission for a picnic. We ride into the field, dismount, unpack the inn's ham sandwiches, and feast. This time I try letting Misty graze on my lead rope at will to see if letting her eat as long as I do will be a good idea. We move around a lot, but it's all across this high field looking over the valley, and it's all lovely. Farther down the slope are several huge pasture conifers with branches to the ground. Under the canopy of one of these trees Pam discovers someone's personal cache of mementos hanging like ornaments, or like votive tokens in a sacred spot.

While he was living here Sanger recovered an older habit of writing fuller journal entries. The entries show some themes. The complicated horse deals, the darker sense of unfair bargains, and the passion for his children's education have appeared in earlier passages. But he revealed more of his feeling for his life as he expanded his journal in the last two years.

To approach what this life may have felt like, the first need is to see what of his pleasures and ordeals reached his record. Abner Sanger did not intend to show a future reader much of either emotion in this journal dedicated to simply keeping track of credits, debts, and barters. Under the surface, one quickly sees that his daily pleasures other than family lay in working the land, in reading, and most of all in good conversations. Just once he mentioned stirring a friend to laughter at his outrageous nicknames, such as "Old Goody Witch Blake" and "Musquash Knowlton."

As for his ordeals, they were ever present, and therefore, routine. Most came from what we would call his "business ineptitude," which seemed to keep him in poverty. He was now adding to his income by boardinglivestock. Still, he spent much of his precious time trying to barter, usually trading work for what he clearly needed. He recorded his failures in short sentences of irony. He went very light in covering the explosions of coming to blows. Pages of his journal show crossed-out passages of anger and frustration. In his Dublin years, mitigating this undercurrent are those passages showing the great love and close care and education he gave his children. One more detail is notable: after frustration, Sanger often closed an entry with a comment on very pleasant weather or moonlight.

I have been assuming that we know what the most destructive challenge of all would have been: the ordeals of this place in winter. But these settlers are not showing that. Instead they show adaptation. Most often, they pass the farm on to one of their children. Editor Lois Stabler comments that "of Sanger's closest friends and neighbors about half left Dublin and moved

Lithograph of drawing by Amos Emerson Dolbear, ca. 1860, "Monadnock from Stone Pond." These northern slopes show contiguous open agricultural lands. [PETERBOROUGH HISTORICAL SOCIETY]

on to Vermont and New York." Not to deny that, but this inquiry shows that a working population stayed on. The successive dates of ownership are showing that when farms changed owners, the farms continued. If we could have ridden along the pair of northern-slope roads we have just finished, Shaker Farm and Old Troy, eighty years later in 1860, at least six of these farms would still be open and active. Artist Amos Dolbear's drawing of these northern slopes in 1860 shows the cleared fields contiguous and extending high up the steeper slopes.[59] Farmers here were working as hard as they could, and on their terms they were making life succeed. Abner Sanger's journal becomes not a record of futile struggle, but an example of making it all work out. He records daily comments about the winter's cold, winds, and storms, and he keeps on going.

To say Sanger showed winter hardiness is an understatement. His descriptions seem to rank the difficulty, but not to stop him. Snow "half a leg deep" did not stop him, nor did "blustery winds" and extreme cold. The only winter conditions that might drive him inside were the "terrible" ones, and they were uncommon, though the winter of 1793–94 brought two of them.

> December 26, 1793. Terrible cold and windy from northeast. Snow drifts all day and night. No traveling.
>
> December 27. Terrible cold and windy from northwest. Snow flies.

It may be unique in the journal that the two adjacent days record no action other than the weather.

But on another unlikely day he was bound to be out.

January 30, 1794:

This morning it appears through the window that the blizzard is finished, though Abner has been saying it was only "very stormy with wind and snow." He has built up the fire, which is crackling in the fireplace and rushing in the chimney, merging with the humming of the eaves from outdoors. Beside the hearth, his and his son's fresh pile of logs from the back dooryard is dripping melting snow from all of its crevices.

In a shaft of light Elizabeth Meed Sanger, seven months pregnant, looks to be feeling better. She and Betsey are chatting while she weaves on the great loom with Betsey's attentions. Their voices can just be heard, under the rhythmic thudding and clicking of wood on wood of the loom. They have little Nabby, healthy again at aged two, playing with a bobbin. Polly Meed, aged sixteen, is sewing, sitting in the second front window light. She is making someone a cape, and six-year-old Hephzy is helping her by keeping the edges together. The room smells of spruce, and baking bread, and the faintly animal scent of new wool.

Now eight-year-old "young Abner" is watching his father, who is peering out front through the whitened windowpanes, toward Monadnock. Abner is reading the mountain. He turns to his boy.

"Andrew Allison is keeping his school. David went out this morning, and he is still there. We can set out."

They haul on all the homespun and leather they have. Now Abner pries up the front door latch. The terrific wind bangs the door wide open to bright light and blowing snow. At the door frame before them, a blue snow wall is full-leg high, and it's blowing into the house.

"Hop on my back. We can set out."

They move out: Abner lunges into the drift. His breath ices, his son's arms and legs are snug around his neck and back. Then he trudges out in "half-leg high" snow—his son is light. David and one other person have left faint tracks, heading down over the best bridge and then straight north. The wind roars from northwest. Allison's school is a bit less than a two miles' walk.

Abner makes progress between the drifts, but in them he wallows. By now the tracks have drifted over. It is the drifts that are concealing the road at full-leg high—at least. Nobody's team has tried to trample the snow. He pauses for breath, plants the boy beside him. He picks him up again, and they struggle on. After about a mile, Abner confesses over his shoulder,

"The snowdrifts are defeating us. But we can get to Deacon Knowlton's."

He turns in to follow a buried farm path, gets to the door, knocks, and they are welcomed, unloaded, warmed, and fed at the Knowltons'. In the afternoon Abner sets out again, much rested and with his son on his back. They make it all the way to school, and once more they are welcomed and rested. Abner stays put at Andrew Allison's school while his son attends the class until it finishes. At night, Abner carries young Abner back home in moonlight. From the woods they can hear the tree branches cracking.

"Very cold night."[60]

In total, Abner Sanger carried his son on his back to and from school, the distance of two miles, his circuit twice a day, for three more days. For the rest of the winter, they all kept moving. These winter days appear to combine ordeal with something like pleasure. What is also striking is that Sanger's phrase "defeat us" is the only phrase I can find in the Dublin journal about weather conditions forcing him to fail to achieve a goal. And his son did not even lose the day.

Then what was it like for the remainder of the year? Are there evident pleasures of working this land? Sanger still, as he did in Keene, recorded working hard at all times of day, every day, and often at night:

> July 24, 1794. Hot and dry. I finish hilling my corn and potatoes east of my barn. Afternoon I begin to hoe in some

> corn, beans, and potatoes southeast corner of my long strip of corn and beans, very weedy with barn grass. Grind scythe at Captain John Morse's (my new flawy scythe). It takes 2 hours in afternoon. We come home. I mow 3 swaths between house and barn. Rhoda's Cooke horse that she rode from Keene gets away in the evening or night.

But there is something more to see. Simply by use of the first-person pronoun, the writer was changing, when compared to his earlier records about tending "Rhoda's farm." These last recorded entries of 1794 show that Sanger was gradually coming to feel that living on this farm was not tending his sister Rhoda's experience but his own, with and for family. Reading these gives a positive feeling. In the sequence below of working across the summer in the same year, we can almost follow him around in our sight as he tended this productive land.

> I sow foul meadow and red top chaff hayseed between the meadow brook and my upland field . . . David Meed and I garden by the highway. Then David destroys worm nests on apple trees. Then we sow parsnips and plant peas. We hedge the garden beds from calves and sheep some . . . Then we cut wood and take care for Sunday. . . I mow the grass above and below my well up to the edge of my orchard. I mow my mustard by the shop, cherry trees and about the woodpile, then mow part of the barn grass on the first sowed piece of flax ground at the right hand as I go to my barn. Afternoon is fair and pleasant.[61]

Working continually, these people had to fight to endure the ordeal of winter's work. And they did it. They could take pleasure in working for its own sake during the summer. My father, who remembered his roots, used to say, "You can make your work your play."

We are beginning to feel the pleasure of our own completed trip easing into our minds. We take our time here, wandering in the field, some of us grazing. In sun and grass, we keep looking toward the azure summit. I set out across the field to lead Misty into the unobstructed perfect view. She and I drift, pausing and walking, over the subtle rise and flattened site until we are standing at the symmetry of dark valley below sharp mountain outline.

When we gather up and prepare to mount again, it is Jack who tells us he wants only his well-deserved grass. He "pulls back," half rearing on his lead line; there's a quick response by both Shelley and Pam, but Jack has stopped first. Jack is warned to remember his training, in no uncertain terms. Misty recalls that my friends will block her if she blocks me, and when I find a grassy hummock for mounting she complies.

We retrace a few steps, re-cross Sanger's bridge, and soon, on Lake Road, ride past the outlet of Dublin Pond. Over a sturdy fence is the rebuilt oldest grist mill, the one Sanger walked to most often, Eli Morse's mill. Eli Morse was still present, but his sons were running it in the 1790s. By then it was one of three mills within Sanger's reach, but the one whose family he knew best. What is not a replica here, but a true relic, is a tavern, a small, wooden one-story house attached in 1822 to the elegant brick

Eli Morse's grist mill, rebuilt, from the 1790s.
[DUBLIN HISTORICAL SOCIETY]

The Eli Morse house about 1885 added to Alexander Scott's wooden tavern of 1758 on the right.
[DUBLIN HISTORICAL SOCIETY]

house beside it. This is Alexander Scott's tavern, on Dublin's branch of an apparent great road and the oldest structure in the town, estimated to have been built in 1758. Alexander Scott must have been a diplomat: this date was still during French and Indian wartime. But much later, Hancock's inn, and before that war, Fort No. 4 in Charlestown had Indian visitors.[62] I would like to hear Scott's stories.

Lake Road is paved, quiet, beautiful among old trees and glimpses of the mountain on one side, and dazzling water on the other. As we come nearer to the end of our trip, the beautiful woodland and filtered views of lake are, in my perception, rolling on by, somewhat like Shelley's video of the undulating scenery. We do not miss the sign that reads "trespassers will be arrested," and keep right on moving. Just before meeting the traffic of Route 101, we can see our turn up Snow Hill Road.

The Eli Morse house, later purchased by Grenville Clark, at the west end of Dublin Lake. Below, Dublin Lake , across from the small mill pond, on which sits Eli Morse's grist mill.
[PAM GODIN]

We can also see, directly across Route 101, a fine squared-colonial white house—the home of Reverend Edward Sprague, Dublin's Congregational minister for nearly forty years, from 1777 to 1818. Historians Leonard and Seward quote from Sprague's eulogy that he was particularly honored for his "pathetic" addresses, funeral sermons, and public prayers. They also note that, having been raised in privilege, Sprague was not good at practical affairs, but because of his inheritance, after 1801 he refused payment for his ministry. They disclose complexity: Sprague was well informed, patriotic, and loved sacred music; later, he tended progressively to commute to Dublin from Keene by coach and four; he had a wit that once aroused could be described as implacable:

> When he had obtained the advantage [in a contest of wit] he was apt to show little mercy. . . . He would give no quarter but press on, and take his own time for ceasing to use his advantage.[63]

Sprague was a friend of Reverend Laban Ainsworth, Jaffrey's beloved minister for the seventy-six years between 1782 and 1858. This is our moment to honor one more pleasure in settlement life: the effects of the regular preaching in their respective towns by the reverends Edward Sprague and Laban Ainsworth. Both were highly educated, with unusually long, honored tenures. Both told stories of a different order from the ones we have been following. Still, one might ask, what happened when these two pastors got together? Leonard and Seward give us a sample.

> A number of clergymen were present one evening at the house of Mr. Sprague; and, while he was out of the room, they began to discuss the question of disinterested benevolence, which, in that day, was a topic of no small interest. Experiencing considerable difficulty in finding a satisfactory example, they agreed to refer the matter to Mr. Sprague for a decision. Accordingly, when [Mr. Sprague] came in, Mr. Ainsworth stated the point of discussion, and the difficulty which they encountered, and requested him to solve the question by furnishing a satisfactory example.
>
> Mr. Sprague quickly replied, "Surely, brethren, I find no difficulty in deciding. I have a case in my mind, a clear and evident one; in short, that must forever settle the question."

Reverend Edward Sprague, Dublin's Congregational minister from 1777 to 1818
[DUBLIN HISTORICAL SOCIETY; JAFFREY HISTORICAL SOCIETY]

Reverend Laban Ainsworth, Jaffrey's Congregational minister from 1782 to 1858.
[DUBLIN HISTORICAL SOCIETY; JAFFREY HISTORICAL SOCIETY]

> But, as he hesitated, and seemed unwilling to state the case or an example, the brethren urged him to proceed.
> "Well," said he, "it is the people of Jaffrey, who pay Brother Ainsworth three hundred dollars a year for preaching, when they do not get, nor expect to get, the least particle of benefit from it. That is what I call pure, disinterested benevolence."[64]

Such in fact is an introduction to the quality of mind, if not to the most characteristic humor, that many of the settlers were listening to, week after week and over the years in those pews. It also shows the kind of wit for which Sprague was known, and it shows that the beloved Ainsworth had a blessedly thick skin.

We turn our horses up Snow Hill Road, which soon becomes gravel, arched by old trees. We turn again to the steeper rise of a private driveway, up to the first hilltop. Then we have been granted use of another driveway, which heads straight downhill onto a dirt lumber trail, on a former road abandoned by 1906. For all of these last choices we have not only owners' permission but encouragement, and a lumber crew has been asked to take the afternoon off.

The lumber trail at first has very soft footing with wheel tracks, but is perfectly navigable. We pass a spring house by a pool in the woods, cross over the furrowed bridge without hesitation, and climb the old road in solid footing along the wooded hillside. One more cellar hole lies beside an old spur trail. The area was once a town-owned lot, and according to the archives holds cellar holes of two houses, this one set aside for use of Jabez Puffer. He was a veteran of the Revolution, wholly crippled by arthritis yet with a family, and the town of Dublin gave him the first "town house." This rectangular foundation is built up quite abruptly on its wide banking of rock, from a drop-off behind it. Abner Sanger watched Jabez Puffer's adult sons coming home for his final days in October 1794. Sanger began an obituary in his journal that depicted Puffer having to sleep in his "great chair" for all of his last years.[65]

Do the horses sense how close we are now to finishing? They have been, and are still, moving flawlessly on. Knowing very well how close we are, I trace two or three more long strokes along the palomino neck that is always in my view. Pam said it: hold on to this day.

The last bit of trail is a true dirt cart path, and many more fallen birch leaves lighten the ground than when we started. Back down Close Road to the junction with pavement that we remember, and after these final eleven miles, we have done it. Everything relaxes. We are rejoicing, at the same time as sliding into the twenty-first century. Cell phones come out: friends will help us home. We take off packs, saddles, and bridles and set them aside—and breathe mightily. The horses begin to nibble contentedly on leaves.

Looking back later on our three days on the mountain with horses, what can we see? For me, the friends and the bonding with our horses in the beauty of this place are still constantly present. And have we gained insight into settlers' lives? I think so. Though we can never experience Monadnock settlement farming, we have touched some fabric of the experience.[66]

Primarily, the insight on the settlers is about physical energy. From today's perspective, settlers' energy seems immense. Over generations we may have forgotten the physical realities of homesteading. In the journal, we can see the settlers working constantly, by hand or by horse plowing the summer's land and the winter's drifts. Mowing, lines of workers swung the scythes. Reaping, they lugged their grain to mills and lugged the flour home. They drove teams, butchered hogs, flayed the carcasses, made shoes, spun, and made clothes. They sowed, hoed, harvested, and stowed, and made up everything they ate for the year. They cleared, built, and maintained home, barn, pasture, the roads, the bridges, the mill, the schoolhouse, the meeting house. They shot wolves, chased livestock, continuing always to fell trees and chop firewood—and all this to stay alive.

A few of us still know this total reliance on physical strength—albeit without the settlers' threshold of survival itself. Peter Sawyer, Jaffrey dairy farmer, well knows this endless, fulfilling work. The collective history of his farm has taught him how, with all effort, to sustain it. But today with independent farming in decline, groups pursuing this level of physical energy are uncommon: the Amish, who collectively hold their traditions, or the dedicated athletes who keep championship ambitions. Monadnock settlers who stayed were perhaps uncommon and certainly self-selected: they chose to keep right on living on a mountain that they had learned

Celebrating fresh leaves and success as we finish on Close Road, Dublin.
[PAM GODIN]

was a place of more severe weather, and narrower flat areas of good soil, than the lands around it.

And the people not strong enough to cope on Monadnock? The historical sources mostly omit them. Showing plenty of drama, these sources do not expand on leaving the mountain, nor on deaths from exhaustion, nor from starvation or freezing or more, nor even the conditions leading that way. Perhaps this is because all the sources focus entirely on living—except for the cellar holes.

We seem to have followed some dedicated pioneers that started it all. The earliest of these settlers—Joseph Brooks, Benjamin Dole, Benjamin Goodenow, Phineas Gleason—took their families farthest from settlements and began living in wooded, or rough-cut, isolation. Each of them later contributed to a fabric of interdependence—of community—that grew around them. They knew that they could live alone, and that next they could create something of wider value.

On their heels came both community growth with sharing of work, and the disadvantages that follow in human interaction. For those, patient and wise counselors and neighbors on both sides of the mountain, Laban Ainsworth, Phinehas Farrar, and Jonathan Hoar, for example, went far toward keeping their respective communities tolerant and positive. John Grout of Jaffrey and Henry Hunt of Marlborough, who each had to be curbed by a crowd, show a converse kind of social strength a new community needed to have.

As for the settlers' pleasures and ordeals, inasmuch as Abner Sanger is representative, much of the pleasure of Monadnock farm life lay in the work itself, and in communal labor. Sanger did not rue mountain life as ordeal, did not blame the weather for his sense of ordeal, but only rued his continual inept trade transactions. His pleasures seem to have been, or to have become, all the rest of life. As one note of confirmation, his wise sister Rhoda, in her will of 1811, left "To my beloved brother, Abner Sanger, the sum of six dollars." She left most of her estate to his twenty-five-year old son who was taking care of him, young Abner.[67]

These records tell us that the settlers on both sides of the mountain saw themselves as succeeding. They did build farms on this mountain. They did adapt. They did grow a community around them. Even on the north side, a number of them passed those farms on as a worthwhile inheritance for at least a couple of succeeding generations of their children, before times changed. They knew what they were doing.

Then there are the emerging roles of the horses. Within these settlement communities, Laban Ainsworth and his bride ride in from Concord, Massachusetts, over fifty miles. John Joslin and the settlers of Ballou City gallop to Richmond and back in a day. Henry Hunt's black colt actually shows adaptation to a tavern remarkably well. Benjamin Goodenow stakes his life on his freight teams. Phinehas Farrar and his horse, as though together, both "want" to be paid. Jonathan Hoar rides to Sudbury, Massachusetts, in February. Abner Sanger weaves trusted horses into the opportunity to keep his children in school.

The best of these horses were essential adapters, every day. They were continually borrowed, so they adapted to people, stayed safe for children. If they were single horses in families they adapted to riding in wilderness, country, and town, then to pack, wagon, sleigh, and work sled. They served along with oxen for hauling, and some of them served just as well for careful transport of children as for joyful speed, year 'round if necessary. This general role is not new, but serves as a testimony to life at this mountain: here is how, farm by farm in the 1790s, horses were enabling the way of life.

And then there is our own horseback experience. Our trail horses, so used to narrower habits, thrived with three days of meeting new locations and experience. Our experiences were mild by contrast, yet we took the horses through hours of woodlands, on forested slopes and timber-cut slopes, onto a highway, into a crowd of children. They traveled all day with no turning home, and then bedded down in wholly contrasting stables. They were more than successful carriers—they were progressively better, beginning each day capable of further harmony with us. Misty gazed at me differently when we completed the ride. Viewed in comparison, our horses' performance echoed the role of their forebears.

Beauty, Jack, and Misty meant far more for us than their overall performance can reveal. We planned them into the center of our experience, and they lived up to it. They served as shapers of our plan, and then steady companions, and cooperative ones. As with all companions, they served occasionally as challengers, subtly as comforts, sometimes as leaders, infrequently as surprises, maybe as clowns. They showed us their complex lives willingly bound with our own.

For me these insights are tactile—even closer than memorable. Distant as we may be from the settlers, we rounded Monadnock on the same earth roads, moving between the bouldered home foundations of a few eighteenth-century people we feel we have met. Our horses engaged us with these people as if time traveling: snug on the backs of their chosen animal, which is our own chosen animal, we trotted into their neighborhoods, we too going somewhere. At times we shared in settlers' comments about their intense politics, their disputes, their horses, the wolves, the bears, and the webworms, and about their children, successes of schooling and arbitration, and the lucky food and fodder from garden and fields on the mountain.

Exploring history and imagination on horseback, from a period when people depended on horses and in a place storied and sometimes demanding, is a powerful experience. It is still resonating—something about endurance, a bonding relationship, and how to make life work out.

SOME WORDS AFTER CIRCLING

PAM GODIN

To ride my horse around Mount Monadnock was just something I will never forget. It will be something that, when I'm in my later years, I will remember fondly and often.

We blended roughing it with glitz. We rode in the rain and stayed in the glamorous and historic Grand View Inn. We rode through fields, along dirt and tar roads, and on my favorite kind of trek, moving for hours through deep woods. We were able to see the extremely hard work our forefathers did in building farms at the mountain, and in their process of building, providing the wonderful roads and trails that we used. It was a beautiful ride, an experience I treasure.

SHELLEY MOZIER

I met Francelia in the spring of 2011. I moved to the barn in Troy where she boarded Misty. We started out with a lot in common: we both had lost our husbands and had an insatiable love of horses. We rode together at least twice a week without fail. In the winter of 2015 we both moved our horses to a barn in Fitzwilliam, where we keep up our riding with new trails to explore.

Last summer Francelia asked me if I would like to join her and Pam in a three-day ride around Mount Monadnock. We would stay overnight at two different inns and would get to explore the trails that the settlers had once ridden. I was thrilled to be included and would do anything to ride my horse.

So, we set off on our adventure. It was wonderful, as Francelia had done research on the cellar holes we would encounter on our ride. She knew all about the families and how many children and how long they stayed. What impressed me the most was how hard life had been to have only horses for transportation and how simply you would have to live, as you can only travel on horseback with limited supplies. It made me appreciate how the settlers must have persevered to live around the base of Mount Monadnock. I am glad I am not a pioneer woman, but to do the ride as we did is an experience I will never forget and I am so grateful—not only for the people who helped us so much to make it happen, but for our three trail horses.

Because of our ride, I now look at stone walls very differently. I look for old caved-in cellar holes and try to imagine how hard their lives were yet how simple they were. The days of traveling only by horseback are over, but for three days we went back in time.

ACKNOWLEDGMENTS

Today's communities of people have helped directly in gathering knowledge about communities two centuries ago, and in making and sharing these new adventures. Continuing support came from Peter and Ann Sawyer and George and Mary Iselin; adding support were Linda Moran, Pam Royce, David Adams, and Jenny Williams.

Among historians and historical societies, invaluable help came from Alan Rumrill and Barbara Bullock Jones, and also from Eric Aldrich and from Lisa Foote, who can restore Dublin fields from forests. Thanks go as well to Karen LaRoche, editor of *Equine Journal*, for publishing a preview of the new ride in 2014. People who knew volunteered extra help: Jason Halliwell most generously, as well as Erlene Lemire, and the Marlborough Select Board. Landowners, often themselves historians, have helped all along: their names are withheld here to protect their privacy. Readers of the manuscript suggested important editings: Alison Clark, Greta Reed, Robert Mason, once again Albert Dole and Bonnie Vendig, and finally Lisa Foote.

Credits for photos, beyond the art by Pam Godin and Shelley Mozier from horseback, include Jaffrey Historical Society and Jaffrey Historic District Commission, Dublin Historical Society, Historical Society of Cheshire County, Monadnock State Park, Peterborough Historical Society, and Jason Halliwell. For the stereoscopic photo of the horse on Monadnock's summit, particular thanks go to Lee Willette.

Map details are from Chester B. Price, *Historic Indian Trails of New Hampshire*, and the "Holland Map" of 1774. Powerpoint was aided by Joel Huberman and Andrea Caldwell.

People at Bauhan Publishing—Sarah Bauhan, Henry James, Mary Ann Faughnan, Cassie Baron, and Jocelyn Lovering—deserve the credit for encouraging this publication, doing it all accurately and beautifully, and making publishing an interactive joy.

Finally, our ground of appreciation: its feature is our three outstanding trail horses who accomplished this for us, but it belongs most deeply to Leo Godin and Tim Austin, who enabled the riders, made room for more work in their own schedules, and helped so much all along.

NOTES

These short references appear in full citation in the lists of Sources and Maps, that follow.

1. This and three subsequent present-tense historical scenes shown in italic are imagined in the present writing, broadened slightly to include some of the details surrounding an original passage of text. The winter night is from an account in Abner Sanger's journal, in Stabler, ed., *Very Poor,* p. 535.

2. The average comparison of Monadnock's weather to its surrounding land is not meant to be a technical one, but simply a thoughtful person's impression. It comes from a Monadnock State Park employee.

3. Discussion of the Abenaki history at Monadnock is from Bruchac, "Sokoki Homeland," in Mansfield, ed., *Mountain,* especially pp. 15–24.

4. Samuel Willard's record of 1725 is in Mansfield, ed., *Mountain,* pp. 10–11.

5. The condensed Colonial history of the Monadnock townships and the Sanger family's place in it comes in part from Lois K. Stabler, "Introduction," in Stabler, ed., *Very Poor,* pp. xx–xxiii. Details on his family show that while Abner Sanger was "poor," he was not "of a low make."

6. Twain's comments on his residencies in a letter, and the inscribed photo, are in Mansfield, ed., *Mountain,* pp. 205–206.

7. Abel Munroe is cited in Leonard and Seward, *Dublin,* pp. 720, 625.

8. On Willard Hunt's move, see Hayward, *Hancock,* pp. 673 and 871. On repeated troubles with Hunt's son Isaac, see Sanger's account in

Stabler, ed., *Very Poor,* pp. 483, 513. But in Hancock after age thirty-three, Isaac Hunt built a reputation of a "wealthy and extensive landowner"; see *Hancock,* p. 674.

9. On Nathan Bixby, in addition to the genealogy in Leonard and Seward, *Dublin,* see "Mountain View Farm," Dublin Historical Resources Inventory, item 19, p. 96. On the use of lame horses noted in Sanger's journal see Stabler, ed., *Very Poor,* for example, p. 506.
10. The junction of roads with houses, brook, and School House No. 4 can be found on Samuel Wadsworth's Map of the Town of Dublin, 1906, Range II, Lot 9, and in its separately bound *Index,* p. 2.
11. The lower portion of Oxbow Road and the discontinued section leading to more house sites and Stanley Brook are on Wadsworth's Map of the Town of Dublin, 1906, Range I, Lots 8 and 7. Its *Index* shows the mill site on Lot 7 number 5.
12. Simeon Bullard's house stood apparently just inside the building complex as the forks leading to Page Road met the Upper Jaffrey Road (Dublin's Range I Lot 9).
13. Kidd's observation is in *Jaffrey Roads,* p. 123. The quotation and the extension of the Gibbs Road past Thorndike's home also appear in Kidd, *Jaffrey Roads,* on p. 111.
14. Discussion of the Ark is in Chamberlain, *Annals,* pp. 28–34.
15. The "Masonian Proprietors" were the owners, and the realtors, of the New Hampshire land available for purchase by settlers. After a century of litigation, the lands once granted by the King of England to Captain John Mason were purchased by a well-to-do group in Portsmouth, New Hampshire, who gave themselves this name. The group, with structured settlements in mind, divided the land into sections with numbered grids of ranges and lots, which they sold. These designations do in fact locate early townships and settlers on the oldest maps, and are the ones used above. The Proprietors also established contact with people local to an area whom they trusted as mid-level agents, or sometimes as buyers who would resell. Abner Sanger's father was one of these.

16. Joseph Brooks and his farm are described in Chamberlain, *Annals,* pp. 17–18, 148–149, and, especially the cellar holes, in Halliwell, *Stories,* pp. 69–70.

17. Tenney, *Sermon,* p. 30. The "Minister's Lot," which was contested in Jaffrey, was part of the pre-planned structure of a township. Grout's challenge to this structure is followed by Chamberlain, *Annals,* pp. 145–147.

18. Abraham Bailey is described in Chamberlain, *Annals,* pp. 149–150. Bailey and the development of the mills are in Halliwell, *Stories,* pp. 81–85; see especially the mill foundations in detail, p. 85.

19. The Royce family history can be found in Chamberlain, *Annals,* in Brandon, *Monadnock,* and through the kindness of Pam Royce.

20. Both stories are in *Annals,* pp. 22–24. Another postscript is on James Ballou. Alan Rumrill writes that Ballou had a wide reputation for foretelling the future, sometimes confirmed his reputation by dressing in the gowns of a wizard, and managed to foretell his own death. His grandson was President James A. Garfield. Rumrill, *Monadnock,* pp. 102, 54.

21. Benaiah Hudson's, and his successor's, farm layout is described in Halliwell, *Stories,* pp. 43–44.

22. The outline of Benjamin Dole's life is from Chamberlain, *Annals,* pp. 141–142. His house site and land, with photographs, is described in Halliwell, *Stories,* especially pp. 39–41.

23. Benjamin Dole and his bear are in Bemis, *Marlborough,* pp. 309–310.

24. For a recent detailed record of the history the Milliken Tavern, see Halliwell, *Stories,* pp. 16–22. It was "Proctor House" and tavern from 1881, when John Ball Proctor bought it, to about 1905. The picture tells us that it was an inn as well.

25. Kidd, *Jaffrey Roads,* p. 103.

26. Both Price's map and Holland's map are shown here in detail. See Price, *Historic Indian Trails.* For Holland's Map of 1784, surveyed in 1774, see Maps, below.

27. The two candidates for great roads on our trip, Old Fitzwilliam Road and County Road in Jaffrey, and Lake Road and Marlborough Road in Dublin, show different signs of their greater age and different use than the smaller roads that connected settlers to each other. The smaller roads, such as Jaffrey's Old Keene Road and Dublin's Shaker Farm and Old Troy roads, run closely past the oldest cellar holes. The former great roads or earliest highways when seen today show misaligned junctions and name changes and may disappear entirely for stretches as their role as military or migratory routes dissolved over time and usages changed. That is the pattern at this junction. (King's Highway, laid in 1768 from Peterborough to Washington, also shows this pattern.)

28. Even the roadbed that is now Old Marlborough Road of Dublin shows generations of "old" when one looks at Wadsworth's 1906 Dublin map. That map shows a discontinued long roadbed branching slightly north but running parallel on slightly higher land just west of Abner Sanger's farm. It is on that discontinued roadbed that Abner Sanger's neighbors on the "highway," Ichabod Rowell, James Upton, one of the Rollins brothers, and Isaac Morse lived. Leonard and Seward mention that the schoolhouse was moved "after the road was altered." Two mapped cellar holes on the present section of Old Marlborough Road, named in the map's Index, date from the 1850s. So a quiet "highway," despite its great age, may not lie in its oldest roadbed.

29. The short history of Horizon Hill Farm is from Jaffrey Center, *Portrait*, p. 145.

30. Research by Eric Aldrich of Hancock has brought Elliot Due to my attention, transforming him from a hazy figure to a tragic one.

31. The military road that MacClintock helped to open or improve in 1760 included the south side of Dublin Pond—apparently, by Holland's Map surveyed in 1774—the Lake and Marlborough roads. See Jones, ed., *MacClintock's Journal*, pp. 16–18. On Sanger's ordeal see also Stabler, ed., *Very Poor*, pp. 80, 152–154.

32. This short description of the Colburn Mills is my layman's summary

of a detailed description kindly supplied in correspondence by Jason Halliwell in 2016.

33. Thoreau's fast hike of September 7, 1852, described in his journal, has been experienced and found sound by Thoreau scholar J. Parker Huber, and that story is in "Following Thoreau," in Mansfield, ed., *Mountain*, p. 89.

34. The historical sketch of The Inn at East Hill Farm is from a telephone follow-up call with the Adams family.

35. Chamberlain characterizes Haskell's Tavern, but, alas, without the stories, in *Annals*, pp. 23, 25.

36. Bemis, writing before 1881 in *Marlborough*, includes the best tavern story I could dream of, as it pertains not only to a horse but to settlers who will become familiar to the reader from Monadnock's northern side. With several sources of material, I have taken the liberty to make this story a present-tense imagined "time-travel" scene, using some terms from Abner Sanger's journal, a few details from knowing a horse who "won't," but almost entirely using the details from the Sweetser's Tavern story from about 1799 in *Marlborough*, p. 192. It seems to be teaching something.

37. Barnes is named by Chamberlain, *Annals*, pp. 18, 155–156, and his house location described more closely by Halliwell, in correspondence, 2016.

38. Richard Davis and his family are described by Chamberlain, *Annals*, pp. 155–157, especially the quotation on p. 157.

39. Abner Sanger's notable passages on Silas are in Stabler, ed., *Very Poor*, on p. 516, 521, 525, 530, 538–539.

40. On the Shaker colony and the Goodenow farm, see Chamberlain, *Annals*, pp. 165–166. Chamberlain misnames Benjamin Goodenow as "William." "Benjamin" is the name consistently used, first by Isaac Wyman (and then by Benjamin himself), quoted in Bemis, *Marlborough*, p. 53, and then by Abner Sanger. See Stabler, ed. *Very Poor*, p. 300.

41. The joke about being ancient Israelites is in Bemis, *Marlborough,* p. 154, and Isaac Wyman's description of Goodenow is in *Marlborough,* p. 53.

42. Bemis, in *Marlborough,* cites Isaac McAlister on p. 24, and Phinehas Farrar on p. 473.

43. Sanger's account of Farrar's apparent arbitration appears in Stabler, ed., *Very Poor,* on p. 506, and of the evening scene, in *Very Poor* on p. 533.

44. Phinehas Farrar's items billed for his services for building the meeting house in 1789, fully listed in Bemis, *Marlborough,* p. 87, are worth reading in full—for variety, for energy required, maybe for subtle humor. The calves' pates, which he and his horse both needed to be paid for fetching, may relate to "sizing" or glutinous material for carpentry.

45. Phillips Sweetser's full recommendation of Farrar for Concord's General Court is in Bemis, *Marlborough,* p. 315.

46. On the value of Monadnock soil on Phinehas Farrar's farm, the owner's comment that it is nutritious has long-time evidence. The soil's value in this region was anticipated as early as in MacClintock's journal of 1760 (see esp. Jones, *MacClintock's Journal,* p. 17), and by Laban Ainsworth in his letter describing Monadnock to Timothy Dwight in 1820. In 1871 the Poole family of Jaffrey returned to farm their Monadnock ancestral land because its possibilities were "fully as promising as the so-called New Jersey fruit land." Chamberlain, *Annals,* pp. 32–33.

47. Leonard and Seward, in *Dublin,* describe Phineas (or Phinehas) Gleason as the first settler on the north side on p. 771. Halliwell describes the immediate farm area in correspondence, 2016. The last date, 1953, which may account for the openness of the site, comes from a conversation. Sanger's comments that relate to Phineas Gleason's hardiness are in Stabler, ed., *Very Poor,* pp. 484, 494, and Gleason's impressive sharing with Sanger of guardianship for David Meed in 1793 is summarized in *Very Poor,* p. 595.

48. The history of Daniel Gleason's house and the trail is from Brandon, *Monadnock,* p. 11, and Chamberlain, *Annals,* pp. 137–38. Because Leonard and Seward list Daniel Gleason as having "emigrated" (p. 954), they decribe him in the Rollins family under the name of his wife, Hannah Rollins Gleason (p. 883). They trace the ownership of his house on p. 625. Daniel Gleason is noted biographically by Sanger's editor Lois K. Stabler in *Very Poor,* on p. 589; the cow transaction is noted on p. 474, the weaving tools, on p. 500, and Gleason's sociability is suggested by three February entries on pp. 494–495. Genevieve Farmer, guide on the Dublin Trail, is described by Henry D. Allison (a descendant of the teacher, Andrew Allison, described on p. 101), in *Dublin Days, Old and New,* and in Thomas Wentworth Higginson's poem from an unidentified newspaper article. Both of these descriptions are provided by the Dublin Historical Society.

49. During the Dublin period of Sanger's journal, 1791–1794, Captain Jonathan Hoar lived in the former Nathan Gleason house on Old Troy Road. Chamberlain, *Annals,* covers Hoar's early lot transactions, p. 138. Lois Stabler covers his marriage to Lucy Gleason, sister of Phineas, in 1783, in *Very Poor,* p. 591. Leonard and Seward's *Dublin* covers his productive reputation in 1796, p. 513. Again, Chamberlain records Hoar's marriage to Betsey Mason, and dates his deed to the house at 1808.

50. That the Nathan Gleason/Jonathan Hoar hall-and-parlor-style home was a large one comes from site observation by Jason Halliwell, 2016. My estimates of its inheritance and duration come from names in Leonard and Seward's *Dublin* and the *Index* accompanying the Wadsworth map of 1906.

51. The activities surrounding Sanger's journal entries here are traceable through the respective dates in Stabler, ed., *Very Poor.*

52. Paul Morse's settlement in approximately 1794 is covered by Chamberlain, *Annals,* p. 138. Abner Sanger's observations of him are in Stabler, ed., *Very Poor,* pp. 522, 535. Morse moved to Maine in

1799, and it was his successor, Amos Emery, who passed the farm on to his son, who in turn held it until 1853. By the beginning of the twentieth century the farm had become a summer home of some seven hundred acres, and its owners gradually moved their focus into major preservation of the higher slopes of the mountain land. (See, for example, Richard Meryman in Mansfield, ed., *Mountain,* pp. 203–204, on this transition.)

53. The quotation from Sanger on meeting Benjamin Mason in 1794 is in Stabler, ed., *Very Poor,* on pp. 525–526. Mason's life is sketched in Leonard and Seward's *Dublin,* pp. 822, 183.

54. "Hurricaned. Felled trees, one atop the other without clearing away afterwards." From the glossary in Stabler, ed., *Very Poor.*

55. The wolf-hunting poem by Ebenezer Morse is in Morse's "communication" to the Centennial celebration of 1852. Morse was sixty-seven in 1852; in 1794 he had been nine. His name "Uncle Ben" was not just a friendly term: his speech includes the elegiac question, "Where are the Morses and the Masons, whose mingled blood flows in my veins?" Leonard and Seward, *Dublin,* pp. 51, 50.

56. The story is converted to present tense for the sake of "time-traveling" immediacy from the telling of the story by Alan F. Rumrill, "Wolves in Croydon," in *Monadnock,* pp. 121–122.

57. In *Dublin,* Leonard and Seward show the admiration of the town over time for the Allison family., e.g., pages 699–703. Sanger's frequent journal entries show his admiration for his favorite teacher, who was also an arbitrator for him.

58. Many of these people's names are known from several sources, but "Eleazer Wilcox and the Bear" is in Rumrill, *Monadnock,* p. 122. My own ambivalent viewpoint on John Kilburn was made clear in my *Time Travel With Horses,* pp. 74-75; Sanger's observations of these people are indexed by their names in Stabler, ed., *Very Poor.*

59. Amos Emerson Dolbear's lithograph *Monadnock from Stone Pond,* from a drawing of about 1860, is shown and discussed in Brandon, *Monadnock,* p. 259.

60. This scene aims to explore the paradox of obvious ordeal and subtle pleasure by converting to present tense the details of the coldest weather, both from personal experience and from the text surrounding, as well as in, Sanger's journal entry of January 30, 1794, in Stabler, ed., *Very Poor,* p. 492. My thanks go to the help of local weavers.

61. Sanger's description of the July 24 working day is in Stabler, ed., *Very Poor,* p. 517. The sequence of summer work spans pp. 510, 511, 525.

62. The Hancock Inn's recurring Indian visitors were remembered in the 1980s by the town's oldest citizen, Bert Manning, as members of logging crews in early twentieth century. The peaceful Indian trading visits to Fort No. 4 as late as 1754 are noted in Calloway, *Western Abenakis,* p. 161.

63. The description of Sprague's implacable humor is in Leonard and Seward, *Dublin,* pp. 234–240.

64. The quoted conversation on benevolence is in Leonard and Seward, *Dublin,* pp. 560–561.

65. Jabez Puffer is in Stabler, ed., *Very Poor,* p. 530.

66. "We have touched some fabric"—though without trying to research why they came. There are studies which take up the complex reasons that colonial farmers moved into New Hampshire and then moved on. Jason Halliwell's recent manuscript, *Stories,* refers to some of the established colonial restrictions on both secular and religious life, citing, for example, Stephen Marini, *Radical Sects of Revolutionary New Hampshire* (Cambridge, MA: Harvard University Press, 1982).

67. Rhoda Sanger's will is in Stabler, ed., *Very Poor,* p. 543.

SOURCES

Allison, Henry D. *Dublin Days, Old and New: New Hampshire Fact and Fancy*. New York: Exposition Press, 1952.

Annett, Albert, and Alice E. E. Lehtinen. *The Generations of Jaffrey, New Hampshire, Arranged After Their Families.* [*History of Jaffrey . . .*Vol. II] Town of Jaffrey, 1934.

Baldwin, Henry I. *Monadnock Guide.* 4th ed., rev. ed. Martha Carlson. Concord, NH: Society for the Protection of New Hampshire Forests, 1987.

Bemis, Charles A. *History of the Town of Marlborough, Cheshire County, New Hampshire.* Facsimile of the 1881 edition. Marlborough, NH: Frost Free Library, 1974.

Brandon, Craig. *Monadnock: More than a Mountain.* Keene, NH: Surry Cottage Books, 2007.

Bruchac, Marge. "Sokoki Homeland from Monadnock: K'namitobena Sokwaki," in Mansfield, ed., *Mountain,* (cited below), pp. 15–27.

Calloway, Colin G. *The Western Abenakis of Vermont, 1600–1800: War, Migration, and the Survival of an Indian People.* Norman and London: University of Oklahoma Press, 1990.

Chamberlain, Allen. *Annals of the Grand Monadnock.* 3d ed., Concord, NH: Society for the Protection of New Hampshire Forests, 1975.

Clark, Francelia, with Pam Godin. *Time Travel with Horses: Exploring Earliest New Hampshire Roads from Peterborough to the Connecticut River.* Printed by Puritan Press, Hollis, NH, 2007.

Clark, Francelia. "Riding the Settlers' Slopes of Monadnock." *Equine Journal.* Fall 2014. Approximately five pages published online.

Cutter, Daniel B. *A History of the Town of Jaffrey, 1749–1880*. Concord, NH: Republican Press Association, 1881.

Halliwell, Jason. *Stories of the Settlers of the South Slopes of Mount Monadnock*. Unpublished manuscript, 2016. Located at Historical Society of Cheshire County, Keene, New Hampshire; Jaffrey (NH) Historical Society; and Dublin (NH) Historical Society.

Hayward, William Willis. *The History of Hancock, New Hampshire, 1764–1889*. Published by the Town History Committee. Lowell, MA: Vox Populi Press, 1889.

Historic Resources Inventory. Collection of Dublin Historical Society, Dublin, NH, 1978.

Hyman, Tom. *Village on a Hill: A History of Dublin, New Hampshire, 1752–2000*. Portsmouth, NH: Peter E. Randall Publisher, 2002.

Jaffrey Center Village Improvement Society, Inc. *Jaffrey Center, New Hampshire: Portrait of a Village*. North Adams, MA: Excelsior Printing Company, 1976.

Jones, Barbara Bullock. *Rev. Samuel MacClintock's Journal, 1760 and Names of Men in Col. Goffe's Regiment*. 2nd edition. Rutland, VT: Crown Point Road Assoc., Inc., Academy Books, 2001. Includes Holland's map (see citation in Maps, below).

Kidd, Coburn. *Jaffrey Roads and Streets 1773–1980*. Jaffrey, NH: Jaffrey Historical Society, 1982.

Leonard, Levi W. and Josiah L. Seward. *The History of Dublin, New Hampshire*. Published by the Town of Dublin. Cambridge, MA: The University Press, 1920.

Mansfield, Howard, ed. *Where the Mountain Stands Alone: Stories of Place in the Monadnock Region*. Hanover, NH: University Press of New England, 2006.

Mason, Edna Warren. *Descendants of Capt. Hugh Mason in America*. New Haven, CT: Tuttle, Morehouse, and Taylor Company, 1937.

Mason, Thaddeus. 1782 papers in the collection of the Dublin Historical Society, Dublin, NH.

Morrison, Leonard A. *The History of the Morison or Morrison Family*. Boston, MA: A. Williams & Co., 1880.

Mountain View Farm. 1978 manuscript in the collection of the Dublin Historical Society, Dublin, NH.

Price, Chester B. *Historic Indian Trails of New Hampshire*. Concord, NH: New Hampshire Archeological Society, 1989. Map.

Rumrill, Alan F. *Monadnock Moments: Historic Tales from Southwest New Hampshire*. Charleston, SC: The History Press, 2009

Squire, Mariella. Lecture and interviews, Keene State College. Keene, NH: Academic year teaching occasions, 1998.

Stabler, Lois K., ed. *Very Poor and of a Lo Make: The Journal of Abner Sanger*. Published for the Historical Society of Cheshire County. Portsmouth, NH: Peter E. Randall Publisher, 1987.

Stephenson, Robert B. and Catherine L. Sieberling. *Jaffrey Then and Now: Changes in Community Character*. Jaffrey, NH: Jaffrey Historic District Commission, 1994.

MAPS

Holland's Map of 1784, with Surveys made in 1773 and 1774, a detail from which appears in Jones, *MacClintock's Journal,* can be found in full in Batchellor, Albert S., ed. *State of New Hampshire Town Charters, Vol XXIV, Town Charter, Vol. I.* Concord, NH: Edward N. Pearson, 1894.

Price, Chester B. *Historic Indian Trails of New Hampshire.* Concord, NH: New Hampshire Archeological Society, 1989. A digital version of the map can be found in the Dartmouth Digital Library Collection under "Price, Historic Indian Trails of New Hampshire."

US Department of the Interior, US Geological Survey (USGS). Adjacent and selected details of topographic map quadrangles. USGS, 12201 Sunrise Valley Drive, Reston, VA 20192, USA. The map selected is from 1949.

Wadsworth, Samuel. Map of the Town of Dublin, from Survey of Thomas Fiske, 1853. Boston: C. J. Peters and Son, Co., Map Makers, 1906. *Index to Map of the Town of Dublin, 1906, By Ranges and Lots,* unsigned booklet, may have been published separately.**NOTES**